The Monkees:
a many fractured image

Scot P. Livingston

ISBN: 1514694638
ISBN-13: 978-1514694633

CONTENTS

INTRODUCTION

The Monkees were not a band. At least they weren't initially. And they were never just a band, even after the TV show ended. The Monkees were never just a TV show either -- otherwise they would've ceased to exist once their show got cancelled. The Monkees were more than a band and more than a TV show; sometimes they were both, sometimes they were neither, but they were always something more. This book, however, will confine itself to the aspect of the Monkees multi-media conglomerate that recorded (and occasionally released) music from 1966 through 1970.

While the Monkees may have initially presented themselves (or been presented) as an autonomous musical unit, that facade was quickly dispelled during the height of their commercial fame. When people found out that that the Monkees "did not play their own instruments," a smaller subsection realized that the actors hired to play the Monkees did eventually lead a palace revolt and became a real live band, much like Pinocchio … or Frankenstein's monster. But even within this schism of the "boys" versus the "executives" there were several different factions within each group, and each had its own take on what the Monkees were supposed to be.

That is the main disadvantage in trying to analyze the Monkees' music as it was released. Usually bands do eventually fracture and split due to evolving "creative differences" between the band members (the most glaring example being The Beatles' *White Album*), but there is at least a common starting ground from which these paths diverge. This is not so with the Monkees. There was not, nor was there ever, any single, solitary vision that began the "band." There was a unifed vision at the outset, but it was not a musical one. The Monkees started as an idea for a TV show by Bob Rafelson and Bert Schneider. Although loosely based on Bob's time as a folk musician, all Bob & Bert wanted musically was "an American Beatles" knowing that would appeal to the network. But other than that, the door was wide open to interpretation as to what the Monkees should actually sound like.

This book is an attempt to separate out the various parties involved in the Monkees' multi-media project into various playlists, and to look at each producer's vision for the "band" to really be able to ascertain the relative worth of each of these *Rashomon*-style viewpoints. While this may be frustrating when analyzing the nine Monkees albums as released by Colgems, Rhino Records has been quite gracious (if occasionally gratuitous) in its reprinting of the catalog by making sure that every last scrap of possible Monkees' music has been released. This provides enough information to reconfigure the albums into lists that match more consistently with each producer's own artistic vision. One of the more enjoyable aspects of the "Monkees as released" is the wide variety of styles and moods that these albums cover. However, by consolidating this variety down to a more coherent version of the "band," we narrow the scope of these releases significantly. I think it is an important and valuable approach to this catalog of music that is already woefully under-appreciated and studied.

I have had to make some choices on which song - or which take of which song - belongs on which playlist. While I have tried to be methodical and precise in these decisions, they are still ultimately my arbitrary decisions and not definitively provable in any way, shape, or form. Also, these lists will be constantly evolving as more information comes to light or as more tracks become available for listening. Certainly I am not saying that all these playlists are necessarily better than the albums that did come out during 1966-1970 (although in some cases, they definitely are). And it is true: the real good stuff is spread out a lot thinner over these playlists, while the actual albums were able to weed out a lot of dross. However, the best of the Monkees material still stands the test of time - and I think placing that material in this new context will give one a better appreciation for these classic tracks.

Now, during the course of compiling these playlists, I did try to set-up some boundaries. I didn't want to be completely subjective and just put together whatever songs I liked for no other reason than that I liked them. On the other hand, since these rules were mine and somewhat arbitrary, I did occasionally bend them. I initially did try to put everything together into album-length playlists, with a side one and a side two, that would've fit onto a piece of vinyl back in the sixties. This worked well for some groups of songs/sessions/producers, but others recorded too little or too much material. That left me in a bit of a quandary. I tried categorizing them as EPs or double albums, or even occasionally singles, but this method eventually got too complicated. Moreover, I couldn't pull off anything as cool as what Michelle66 did with her alternate Monkees' history at http://www.ipernity.com/doc/302599/album/605301

Half of the fun of being a Monkees fan is playing armchair quarterback and creating your own alternate, superior version of each Monkees LP. One could even try arranging solo tracks either pre- or post-Monkees in order to create more hypothetical albums. While this can be interesting and fun, the indifferent and/or infrequent solo output of all of the Monkees (except for Mike) makes it difficult to do very much with this mental exercise.

What I did do was break everything apart into groups by producer (the actual producer and not necessarily the one credited on the official release). From there I tried to carve out playlists from songs that were recorded around the same time. This could get a tad confusing and sometimes I had to use my best judgment. For example, there was might be a series of sessions that produced eight tracks in February -- which would constitute one playlist -- and another group recorded in November of that year, which would be the next playlist. But what if there was one or two tracks recorded in between these sessions? Would they be included with the first batch or the second? Or would they have to have their own separate tiny set-list? These are judgment calls I would also have to make and will try to justify throughout this tome.

Once I grouped everything into their respective playlists I then put the songs in chronological order. This is not often the best way to listen to these songs, and I would recommend either putting each playlist on random or finding a song order of your own that flows better. However, for purposes of the book, I felt that the best way to list these songs was by date. This also occasionally presented problems. Sometimes several songs were recorded on the same day, so I would have to put them in an order that made sense to me. Other times some songs would be started during one session -- but not completed until several years later. Do I count these songs as part of the group that they started with, or the one where they were finally done? Would I try to find a mix or version of the song that did not have any non-contemporaneous overdubs to try and keep the purity of the playlist intact? Or would I use the most finished version, knowing it was complete and sounded better? In some cases not all versions may have been actually available for release alongside the other tracks recorded during the playlist.

I ended up choosing to organize songs based solely on the date they were started (this is noted on the playlists) -- but to also use the most finished versions, as they were probably going to get there eventually; they just didn't have time at the moment. Also, it is far easier and entertaining to listen to a song that isn't missing obvious elements (such as lead vocals). Of course, when the difference is a mere three or four years, the difference isn't that notable, but in the case of the backing tracks that were finished up

3

in 2016 for the album *Good Times!* you can't really ignore the difference between a 20 year-old's voice and a 70 year-old's. Still for consistency's sake I decided to keeps the songs grouped together by when they were first started.

Another problem I encountered: Some songs were recorded two (or three or four) times. In these cases, I would have to decide whether to keep all the different versions in their own playlist, and if not I would have to decide which version to keep. In general, I decided to only keep one version of each song, just to keep the size of these playlists down and keep the scope of this book manageable. Occasionally, if there was a big enough difference between the two versions, I would keep them both -- but usually, I only kept one. And in general, I tended to keep the earliest version, as that was probably closer to the original author's intent -- even if the later version was the one more people are familiar with – and even if, in some cases, the version that is superior (although typically the earlier draft tended to sound better one to me).

There are also numerous different mixes in both mono and stereo of each song (take a look at http://monkeesmixography.wikidot.com if you don't believe me). While these variations may be of interest to extreme audiophiles; for the average listener, myself included, these all tend to sound the same so I haven't bothered noting which mix of particular song I was using and would encourage you to use whichever one you like best, or have access to.

Please note that the musicians' credits I have included are only accurate to the best of my ability. Documentation wasn't always paramount during this period, especially considering how little credit the session musicians were given during the time of these albums' original release. I have mostly included them to give you an idea of how many different instruments were being played and by how many different people were involved and whether or not these were the same people who played on other sessions in this book.

Once I had compiled all of my playlists, I then had to decide how to arrange them within this book. Going chronologically was going to be an issue as there were often two or even three producers working on their own sessions simultaneously. Instead I decided to group together all of the playlists by production team together into their own chapter. This does tend to make the storyline quite confusing as most producers were initially hired at the start of the show, to be summarily sacked at the height of The Monkees' success, only to be sheepishly asked back when their fortunes flagged in hopes of recalling past glories. While this does make the overall plot of the various Monkees' producers coming and goings harder to keep track of, I think it helps present a clearer picture of each producer's own vision or perspective on the Monkees.

4

For those who are not as familiar with the whole Monkees story, I will briefly outline it here. Inspired in part by his adventures as a folk musician and by the phenomenal success of the Beatles' *A Hard Day's Night* aspiring filmmaker Bob Rafelson teamed with Bert Schnedier (who happened to be the son of Abraham Schneider who ran Screen Gems TV for Columbia pictures) and concocted the idea for a sitcom about a band of struggling musicians and the wacky misadventures. Initially, they were going to hire an already established band (The Loving Spoonful was seriously considered at one point) to star in this pilot, but eventually Bob & Bert decided to hire actors to play the parts of the members of this fictitious band and placed an ad in Variety.

However to keep things interesting - or confusing - they did not first create characters for these actors to audition for - instead they were going to create characters around the people the cast - and even name these characters after the actors who were playing them. Already the lines between real and fake were become a bit fuzzy. After a long series of grueling auditions (from which Stephen Stills, Van Dyke Parks, Paul Williams, and Charles Manson reportedly did not make the cut) Bob and Bert decided on their foursome. They created a group that would generate good drama and chemistry on-screen but never would've come together on their own in real-life due to their very different backgrounds and temperaments.

Since these four were not in any way, shape, or form a band, Bob & Bert needed someone to create the actual music for the pilot in order to sell the show to NBC. That is where Bob & Bert hired young songwriters and producers Tommy Boyce and Bobby Hart for the job. Bob & Bert had either implicitly promised or implied to Boyce & Hart that they would get to do the music for the TV show once it got picked up. Of course, Bob & Bert did not have the authority to actually make that promise as NBC was going to hire someone with a little more experience and track record as hit-makers if they actually decided to produce and air *The Monkees* TV show. Of course, Rafelson and Schneider were not above making these suggested but not stated promises in order to get their show made. They had already hinted to the naive Peter Tork that once the cast got good enough they could be musicians on the records as well as telling the temperamental Michael Nesmith that he would also get to produce music for the show.

To helm the Monkees' music, NBC had originally wanted such hot producers as Mickie Most, who turned them down, and Snuff Garrett, whose lone session for The Monkees was such a disaster that he left the project. However, as they were unable to find anyone in time, the Powers-That-Be (to borrow a phrase from Micky Dolenz's autobiography) relented and let Boyce & Hart produce most of the first album with a pair of tracks done by Michael Nesmith thrown on there for good measure. Mostly NBC just wanted to get something out as quickly as possible in order to promote their new show. That probably assumed that the TV show is where they would make their real money. They probably assumed that the records would be competing more with the likes of the soundtracks to *Green Acres* or *Bewitched* rather than actually rivalling the Beatles or the Stones.

However once that first album became a huge hit, NBC definitely wanted to keep that golden goose producing and so hired music supervisor Don Kirshner. Don Kirshner was not a man with any actual musical ability -- or even musical taste. What Don Kirshner had made his fortune on was being "The Man With The Golden Ears". No one was better able to pick out which song would be a massive selling record like Don. He did not care if the song was actually any good or not, he knew what would sell. He was good at it and was extremely proud of the fact.

So while all of this was going on behind the scenes, the four cast members of the Monkees had been together long enough to learn how to play together as an adequate garage band. Which they were encouraged by the Powers-That-Be to do in order to have them generate more money by way of concert tours. While the "band" was out playing concerts in front of thousands of people, they reasonably assumed that they would somehow be involved in the making of the second record. Meanwhile Boyce & Hart, assuming their success on the first record would allow them a similar amount of control on the second record, were busy working on their own record in L.A. All of this was for naught however, as Don Kirshner (who was based out of New York and hated to fly) was busy having the biggest names of the day working on tracks as well - tracks that everybody assumed were just for the TV show and not for the actual records.

So both Boyce & Hart, as well as the four Monkees, must've been surprised when a second album, entitled *More Of The Monkees* came out. The album which featured some very self-congratulatory liner notes by Don Kirshner himself, collected a requisite pair of Nesmith tracks (one of which Mike didn't sing on), a mere two songs recorded by Boyce & Hart, and some extremely commercial but cheezy material cut by the likes of Carole King & Gerry Goffin, Neil Sedaka, and Don Kirshner's personal favorite Jeff Barry. The underhanded nature of this release particularly irked Mike (who wanted control of the music) and Peter (who wanted to be in a real band). This led to the now infamous incident where Michael punched his fist through a wall and blew the whistle to the press on the fact that the Monkees didn't actually play their own instruments on the records. This led to an unexpected blowback by the hipper-than-thou press who already resented the Monkees for what they felt was an unearned amount of success.

Mike and Peter galvanized the two other actors on the show to essentially unionize and demand a role in the record making process. The

Powers-That-Be, who didn't want to jeopardize their record sales, promised the boys that they could be musicians on the b-side of the next single. Don Kirshner, however, saw this as an affront to his power and control over the Monkees project, and went ahead a released a single - just in Canada - without the promised b-side. While NBC didn't want to rock the boat that was making them so rich, the conflict had come to a head. The Powers-That-Be figured it would be a lot easier to replace Don Kirshner than the four now famous actors, and fired Kirshner, paving the way for the Monkees themselves to actually make their own music.

But the Monkees were not allowed to produce their own music, so on Mike's suggestion they hired Turtles bassist Chip Douglas, despite (or perhaps because) he had never actually produced a record before. Together the five of them worked really hard and produced a charmingly rough and home-made feeling album entitled *Headquarters*. This album sold well (being kept out of the #1 spot all summer by the Beatles' *Sgt. Pepper*) but not nearly as well as the last two. It was also a lot of work. Davy, who mostly joined along with the other three out of solidarity (and a fear that he'd lose his plum gig) certainly didn't care if he played tambourine on the next album or not. Micky, who was initially a lot more enthusiastic about the split with Kirshner, had gotten bored with playing drums and simply opted out of the next album. This left Mike and Peter with Chip Douglas and session drummer Eddie Hoh to record *Pisces, Aquarius, Capricorn, & Jones Ltd.* at various stops during their tour in support of *Headquarters*.

Once that album was done however, the Monkees who no longer had the common enemy of Don Kirshner, found they didn't have any common ground musically and each decided to split off and record their own tunes for themselves which would later be compiled by the far more amenable, but less interested, Lester Sill. The first album that Lester Sill put together was the incongruous mish-mash entitled *The Birds, The Bees, & The Monkees* - sessions for which were held at the same time as the sessions for their next venture the soundtrack for their new movie, *Head*. To make things even more confusing, the album after this, *Instant Replay*, is made up mostly of leftovers from these sessions, so that all three of these albums rather hard to separate out as they generally overlap. With all four Monkees working separately there was a <u>lot</u> of material recorded during this period, a good portion of which didn't get released on either of those three albums.

It was also during this confusing period that the Monkees and NBC decided mutually to end the TV show after the second. Without the TV show that was initially their sole reason to be together, the four guys, along with Bob & Bert, decided that they were going to make movies, starting with the underrated masterpiece *Head*. Perhaps Bob & Bert were deliberately undermining the project in the hopes of getting to do something else for a change, but *Head*, as great as it was, was the exact opposite of what the Monkees fans wanted. Confusing, dark, surreal and psychedelic, *Head* quickly ended the Monkees' popularity. The film was too trippy for the Monkees' usual younger audience, and the Monkees were too much of an anathema amongst the stoned hippies that would've appreciated the film at the time.

Head's distinctly ant-commercial bent along with the much weirder music they were releasing did a lot to derail the gravy train, but the lack of a TV show every week promoting their new records was the main culprit in ending the Monkees as a money-making enterprise. Yet despite this, The Monkees continued to limp along. First there was a TV special called *33 ⅓ Revolutions Per Monkee* that was just as weird as *Head* but not a tenth as good. This got critically and commercially savaged. Next Peter left the group; which considering how little his work was added to the released output of the Monkees shouldn't have hurt them too considerably; but it definitely showed the cracks on the facade. There was initially talk of a double-album entitled *The Monkees Present* with each one of the Monkees taking their own side so they wouldn't have to try to integrate these disparate styles into a cohesive whole. Unfortunately with the departure of Peter Tork, *The Monkees Present* was released as just another hodge-podge of new tracks and old outtakes very similar to the previous album, the appropriately titled *Instant Replay*.

Soon after that, Mike saw the writing on the wall and bought his way out of the contract. With the two troublemakers gone, Jeff Barry was brought back into the fold to try and revive that old Monkees' magic. Despite the fact that their reruns were now big hits on Saturday morning TV, The Monkees' 1970 album as a duo, *Changes*, was a huge flop and soon Micky and Davy went their separate ways.

Almost as soon as the Monkees broke up they began having resurgences. In 1969, the TV show which had been deemed so radical and daring when it debuted three years ago, was now airing as reruns for children on Saturday morning. Almost like clockwork, every ten year anniversary of the show resulted in a new wave of interest. In the mid-1970s, Davy and Micky were unable to recruit Peter or Mike in their first excersize in nostalgia. Instead, they settled for the next best thing: Tommy Boyce and Bobby Hart. Billed as "The Guys Who Wrote 'Em and The Guys Who Sang 'Em" they recorded an album entitled *Dolenz, Jones, Boyce & Hart* and toured through Japan.

With the 20th Anniversary in 1986, The Monkeees once again found themselves in the spotlight. A young MTV, whose creation in fact owes some debt to an entrepreneurial Michael Nesmith, began a 22 ½ hour marathon of the TV show. This led to an amazingly successful reunion tour featuring just Micky, Peter, and Davy and a far less successful album entitled Pool It! Nez was too busy being a music video pioneer, movie producer, and cantankerous old coot to join in the album and all by a one-off appearance on the tour. This renewed spike in popularity also led to the New Monkees. Their syndicated TV show lasted one season and they did record one CD, but about whom the less said the better.

By the time the 30th Anniversary rolled around, Michael set aside his differences and we have the last gasp of activity from the Monkees as a foursome. First the was the album *Justus*. Clearly Mike, Davy, Micky and Peter still had a chip on their shoulder about the criticism they received. However, what they didn't have was a Chip Douglas in the studio. Not only did they play all their own instruments, but they produced the records themselves and wrote every song. The Monkees also managed to briefly return to television with an all-new hour-long special written and directed by Michael Nesmith. All four Monkees even made a brief tour of England before in-fighting led Nez to retreat back into his hole.

The 40th Anniversary occurred during one of those times when there failed to be a quorum of Monkees who were getting along well enough to make any new music. Since it is only the music and not the personal squabbles that this book is interested in this is of little consequence. However Davy, Micky and Peter managed to patch things up in time for a 45th Anniversary tour, shortly after which Davy died of a heart attack on February 29th, 2012.

Given Mike's general discomfort with the Monkees project, even during the sixties, one could safely assuming that the passing of Davy would also mean the end of the Monkees. No one would've expected that the somewhat agoraphobic Michael Nesmith would in fact join Micky and Peter as the Monkees for three tours of the US from 2012 – 2014. Even with Mike's surprise re-emergence as a performing artist, no one would've expected that the 50th Anniversary would manage to coax a new album out of the group.

The band's first reunion album, *Pool It!* Was recorded much in a similar vein as the Monkees' debut album. Both were produced almost exclusively by one outside producer with simply vocals added – except for two songs forced on there by the most musically involved member of the group at the time; Mike in the 60s and Peter in the 80s. Their second reunion album, *Justus* was recorded much like *Headquarters*, only to the nth degree. No outside songwriters or producers this time, just the four of them. Their third reunion album, *Good Times!*, is actually assembled more like their post-*Head* albums, with some old songs dusted off and thrown on there, a few new recordings, and a new version of an old unreleased Boyce & Hart tune. I'm a little reticent to call *Good Times!* the Monkees' final, album, since I have been wrong on that before, but I think I should have some time before anything else new gets recorded.

It may be a little hard to all keep track of, but that is how the official albums that were released by the Monkees - or at least under the Monkees' name. From here, I'd like to go back and pick them apart; rearrange the songs and see if I can't take the mosaic that was the Monkees and put them back into their original places.

BOYCE & HART 1

1.) (Theme From) The Monkees 2:18*
(written by Tommy Boyce and Bobby Hart)
from The Monkees debut album
July 5th, 1966

2.) This Just Doesn't Seem To Be My Day 2:06*
(written by Tommy Boyce and Bobby Hart)
from The Monkees debut album
July 5th, 1966

3.) Let's Dance On 2:30*
(written by Tommy Boyce and Bobby Hart)
from The Monkees debut album
July 5th, 1966

4.) I'll Be True To You 2:46*
(written by Gerry Goffin and Russ Titelman)
from The Monkees debut album
July 9th, 1966

5.) Take A Giant Step 2:28*
(written by Gerry Goffin and Carole King)
from The Monkees debut album
July 9th, 1966

6.) Saturday's Child 2:41*
(written by David Gates)
from The Monkees debut album
July 9th, 1966

7.) I Wanna Be Free 1 [Fast Version] 2:49
(written by Tommy Boyce and Bobby Hart)
first released on *Missing Links Vol. II*
July 19th, 1966

8.) I Wanna Be Free 2 [Slow Version] 2:23
(written by Tommy Boyce and Bobby Hart)
from The Monkees debut album
July 19th, 1966

9.) Tomorrow's Gonna Be Another Day 2:36
(written by Tommy Boyce and Steve Venet)
from The Monkees debut album
July 23rd, 1966

10.) Gonna Buy Me A Dog 2:39
(written by Tommy Boyce and Bobby Hart)
from The Monkees debut album
July 23rd, 1966

11.) Last Train To Clarksville 2:44
(written by Tommy Boyce and Bobby Hart)
from The Monkees debut album
July 25th, 1966

12.) I Can't Get Her Off My Mind 2:48
(written by Tommy Boyce and Bobby Hart)
first released as a bonus track on The Monkees' debut album
July 25th, 1966

13.) (I'm Not Your) Steppin' Stone 2:22
(written by Tommy Boyce and Bobby Hart)
from More of the Monkees
July 26th, 1966

UNFINISHED SONGS FROM THESE SESSIONS:
Whatever's Right (written by Tommy Boyce and Bobby Hart)

Produced by Tommy Boyce and Bobby Hart, except
*Produced by Tommy Boyce, Bobby Hart, and Jack Keller

MUSICIANS:
WAYNE ERWIN, GERRY McGEE & LOUIE SHELTON: guitars
LARRY TAYLOR: bass
BILLY LEWIS: drums
GENE ESTES: tambourine, percussion, mallets, maracas
BOBBY HART: organ, tack piano, autoharp
TOMMY BOYCE: acoustic guitar
MICHEL RUBINI: organ (on "I Wanna Be Free 1"), harpsichord (on "I Wanna Be Free 2" and "Take A Giant Step")
BONNIE DOUGLAS & PAUL SHURE: violin (on "I Wanna Be Free 2")
MYRA KESTENBAUM: viola (on "I Wanna Be Free 2")
FREDERICK SEYKORA: cello (on "I Wanna Be Free 2")
JACK KELLER: piano (on "Take A Giant Step")
MICHEL RUBINI: harpsichord (on "Take A Giant Step")

BOB COOPER: oboe (on "Take A Giant Step")
JOSEPH DITULLIO: cello (on "This Just Doesn't Seem To Be My Day")
TOMMY BOYCE, BOBBY HART, RON HICKLIN, WAYNE ERWIN, MICKY DOLENZ, PETER
    TORK, & DAVY JONES: backing vocals

Recorded 7/5/66 - 7/26/66

This playlist comes closest to the actual released album. This is pretty much the Monkees' self-titled debut album with Mike's two (stand-out) tracks replaced by the only two actual outtakes from Boyce & Hart's sessions. The released album is pretty close to what Bob Rafelson and Bert Schneider may have promised in order to get the pilot made: creative control for Boyce & Hart with creative input for Michael Nesmith.

The sound of the Monkees here is far more the sound of the Candy Store Prophets, Boyce & Hart's backing band. This was not a "real" band in their own right; they were also not an unconnected group of anonymous studio musicians. The fact that they had played together a lot, and were sort of limited technically, but had more personality in their playing, did add to the illusion that the Monkees were a real band on the first album. Although the sound wasn't as stripped down and self-contained as a single band would've been it's still pretty raw. The Candy Store Prophetswere augmented by two session guitarists, Louie Shelton and Wayne Erwin, which made the end result far more polished than an actual debut by a self-contained unit ever would've been.

"(Theme From) The Monkees" is a great tune to start with. Not only is this song a perfect opening for both the TV show and the debut album, but it also illustrates two common traits in Boyce & Hart's work, one of which was their ability to be inspired by, or steal from, what was hot on the charts at the time. Sometimes they did it subtly like swiping the shufflin' finger-snappin' tempo and feel from the Dave Clark Five's "Catch Me If You Can." Sometimes it's a little more blatant and lazy, as seen in the song "Me Without You" which is an almost blatant plagiarization of the Beatles' "Your Mother Should Know."

The other motif of Boyce & Hart's that this song employs is the "guitar solo." I put this in quotes, as it is not a guitar solo in the fashion that we usually hear with one lead guitar improvising a melodic line by itself. Rather, Boyce & Hart preferred (perhaps because they were uncertain of the improvisational abilities of their studio musicians/backing band) was one guitar playing one riff over and over, then another guitar playing a completely different riff repeatedly. While all of this was happening, the rest of the band got louder and more frenzied till the lead vocalist, usually Micky, let out a scream. This was what Boyce & Hart often used in place of a traditional guitar solo and it is used it here quite effectively. While the truncated TV version of the theme may skip this part of the song, it is as an anthemic statement from Boyce & Hart about the band as lyrics about "being the young generation" and "not putting anybody down."

While the Theme Song is a pretty straightforward piece of rock, their next number, **"This Just Doesn't Seem To Be My Day"**, is a much more ambitious production. As was the initial tendency with almost all of the producers who worked with the Monkees, Micky was given the faster, more rock-type of songs while the slower, more ballad-like songs were usually reserved for Davy. This may not have had anything to do with Davy's inability to deliver the harder-edged stuff as much as it was to play up his romantic role on the TV show and give the screaming teenage girl audience what they were clamoring for.

It starts off with a pseudo-exotic sounding intro that I think is supposed to be somewhat Indian, aping George Harrison's latest excursions with the Beatles. From there it breaks into a much more straight-forward pop-rock song. After two verses of Davy decrying his bad luck, we get to a bridge section with some faux-classical overtones as the drums drop out and we are greeted with harpsichord and cello. There are now two different Davy vocals going on at the same time with one of them doing a semi-sophisticated counterpoint part. From here we go back to another verse before having a repeat of the intro section which segues perfectly back into the bridge. We get another verse before fading out on a repeat of that initial foreign-sounding introduction. Any one of these otherwise incongruous elements might've become cloying had they been stretched out to a full-song length, but having them all intersect in some sort of kaleidoscope makes this one of the most ambitious tracks that Boyce & Hart have tried. Luckily the Candy Store Prophets are up to the challenge and this track comes off as one of the best on this playlist.

"Let's Dance On", however, is about as simplistic and straight-ahead as a song could get. One of the many styles that the Monkees' project has dabbled in and become known for is the garage rock that later spawned punk and grunge. It is no surprise that the Sex Pistols covered a Monkees song, and when they did it was one written by Boyce & Hart. While sometimes Boyce & Hart's loftier goals remained a tad out of their reach, when they were producing and writing this type of four-the-floor dance number with no brains required, that is when they were at their best. This song is definitely one within that wheelhouse. It may not have a lot to say or mean anything other than "have fun", but still it is a damn fine rock'n'roll song, one whose simplicity actually contributes to its longevity. While not terribly flashy or even especially memorable this song is overlooked and deserves to be re-evaluated.

While "Let's Dance On" is the epitome of rock, **"I'll Be True To You"** represents the other style of music that Boyce & Hart did a lot of, only not nearly as successfully. Since it is a slower romantic song, of course it is sung by Davy. One of the big reasons that Davy was hired on at the Monkees is because he was English, which thanks to the Beatles was all the rage at the time.

However, the stuff the Boyce & Hart gave Davy to sing wasn't so much Beatlesesque as it reminded one of another popular contemporary British artist, Herman's Hermits. This is the kind of faux-music hall number that is cheeky without ever getting scary enough to be offensive to even the stuffiest parents. This was a safe fake rebellion for little girls who wanted to pretend to grow up but didn't want to hurt Mommy and Daddy. Like so many teen idols before him and since him, Davy was popular because he was non-threatening. And this song is the essence of that. You expect Davy to pull out a straw hat and cane and do a soft-shoe routine during this song. Unlike the last tune, which had some vitality to it, this track feels calculated and mercenary; and while Davy sincerely loved entertaining and does his best to sell it, this track just comes off as crass. Not that this is entirely Boyce & Hart's fault since this one of the few tunes that they produced that they did not write, perhaps trying to gain the trust of Don Kirshner and the Powers-That-Be that they could do stuff that they felt was commercial as well.

The next song was also co-written by Gerry Goffin, this time with his much more famous partner, Carole King. **"Take A Giant Step"** has oddly become a favorite of Peter Tork's as he recorded a banjo version of it on what is still his only solo album, 1994's *Stranger Things Have Happened.* This version is much more in the vein of the other tracks here. In some ways this song is just a lesser version of "This Just Doesn't Seem To Be My Day." Like that track this one starts off with a bit of attempted exotica; however it isn't as convincing or distinctive. There again attempts to blend this with a more straight-forward verse, but this song flows a lot more seamlessly because it just doesn't feel very different to begin with. The best part of this tune comes at the end with the toms drumming up a cool budda-budda-bum-bum as the song begins to fade out. Still it's nice to see that even this early on, Boyce & Hart were trying to expand the Monkees' musical palette beyond the simple teeny-bopper stuff that they were most often associated with.

Peter was initially enlisted to sing lead on **"Saturday's Child"** but unfortunately no tapes of that attempt have yet surfaced. It would've been interesting though to see Boyce & Hart try to find a way to utilize Peter somewhere in their songs. I'm sure as a cross-promotional marketing tool, NBC would have loved to have all four Monkees singing at least one song on the album, but nobody (including Peter himself) ever really seemed to know what to do with his voice. And while Lennon & McCartney figured out a way to utilize what Ringo Starr brought vocally at least once per album, the Monkees always were stumped when it came to Peter. A lot of problem was that unlike the other three Monkees, there was a distinct difference between the type of person that Peter Tork was in real life and the type of character he played on the TV show. Oftentimes producers were uncertain which Peter Tork to try and tailor their stuff for and as a result he ended up having very few lead vocals, released or unreleased, in the Monkees' catalog.

As it is, "Saturday's Child" is just another rock song for Micky to sing, although it's a little more mid-tempo than what he had usually sung. While there's nothing particularly grand or interesting to discuss about this song it is very catchy and solidly played by the Candy Store Prophets. The lyrics are half-cryptic pseudo-astrology, but as usual are confined to the same subject matter as every other song on this playlist: romantic boy/girl love songs. While not super-energetic, this is still pretty good rocking song. Keep in mind though that this was written by David Gates, who later went on to work in one of the wussiest soft-rock bands of the 1970s ever... Bread.

I know I had said earlier that I was going to try and avoid having the same song appear in two different playlist, and I usually stuck by that. This however is the only time that the same song appears twice in the same playlist; but there's a good reason for that. **"I Wanna Be Free"** was recorded in two versions (on the same day) that really demonstrate the difference between Boyce & Hart's two main modes of production and their two schools of thought associated with either Davy or Micky. The first version, which was used in the pilot, is an up-tempo rock number with a prominent organ that reminds many people of Bob Dylan's work at the time. This version is sung primarily by Micky with a lot of help from Davy. The second version, which is the version that came out on the record, is much slower and is clearly modeled on the Beatles' "Yesterday" having just an acoustic guitar with strings behind it. This is the version that Davy sings lead on.

While the song is still the same melody and chords and lyrics in both versions, they each feel completely different. The fast version is defiant and confident with hints of vulnerability peeking through the cracks. The slow version is pleading and whiny, and comes across as a little creepy. Actually both versions are rather hamstrung by the lyrics in which our commitment-phobic narrator is pleading with the object of his desire to essentially let him have his cake and eat it too. He wants her to stand beside him, but he doesn't want to be chained down to her. It is a slightly depressing, misogynistic sentiment that mars an otherwise solid tune. Although the sappy ballad-version of the song almost becomes unlistenable once you know that there's the other, much better, version that could've and should've come out on the debut record, neither one is a real dud.

"Tomorrow's Going To Be Another Day" is almost a folk-rock tune with its "hey hey hey"'s and the harmonica at the end of the usual Boyce & Hart guitar solo. The opening riff sounds like an early rough draft of what would eventually become "Last Train To Clarksville", but isn't quite all the way there yet. It's another fun catchy upbeat tune that makes for a great album track. Not exactly filler, but not single material either, it is definitely a good fit for both the album and the TV show.

While the TV show was undeniably a comedy, none of the records released under the Monkees' name were really considered funny or novelty records. Very little of the show's funny ad-libbed spirit actually made it into the music, which was always played straight so as to appeal to the pop music buying audience. However there is one big exception to that rule, and that is **"Gonna Buy Me A Dog"**. The track is what it sounds like; namely Micky and Davy attempting to sing the song that they've never heard before while making jokes and screwing up and generally having a good time. Clearly, this was also supposed to be a joke-y tune with the bits about Zulus and necks leaking being scripted out in advance. But Micky and Davy are having a lot more fun with it than just that. First off, neither one seems real impressed with the song. Secondly, they clearly don't think that anyone is ever going to hear this take. They just don't care here, and it is fun and infectious. It shows a great deal of savvy coupled with some humility for Boyce & Hart to have not erased that take immediately much less saved it to be released on the album. I'm sure there is a take out there of the two of them doing an actual straight job of singing this song - and had that been released this would've been one of the weakest tracks on this playlist. As it is, this is still one of my all-time favorite Monkees' songs ever.

Going from the silly to the sublime, the next song is **"Last Train To Clarksville"**. While the question is often asked: did the records sell because the TV show was a hit or was the TV show a hit because the records sold? It's hard to say. On one hand, once the TV show went off the air, the hits stopped coming. On the other, this song was a hit before the TV show debuted. The Monkees do tend to be regarded as more of a singles band than an album group and this is certainly the first and one of the biggest of those singles that this reputation is built on. It is a supremely solidly constructed pop-song. The way that the hi-hat mimics the sound of a train is ingenious. The opening guitar riff is infectious. The whole song is apparently modeled after a mis-hearing of the fade-out of the Beatles' "Paperback Writer".

Personally I don't go bananas for "Last Train To Clarksville" the way that some people do, perhaps because it is just a little too good and perfect and I prefer something that might be a little rougher but feel more human. Not that "Last Train To Clarksville" is too professional or polished, but it does seem put together exactly the way it should be with the usual non-solo guitar solo and the vaguely, but non-explicitly, anti war lyrics. There's a reason why this is a hit, and who am I to argue with it? I certainly don't turn this song off when it comes on the radio (which happens quite a bit, unlike say "Tapioca Tundra"). But this is also not a song I would queue up and play very often on my own.

"I Can't Get Her Off Of My Mind" is the only real outtake that Boyce & Hart produced for the Monkees' first record. This track was probably left off since there was already one kitschy music-hall pastiche on the album and they didn't need another. Inexplicably, this song was revived by the Monkees themselves once they took over the reins of recording. Perhaps because Davy wasn't writing his own material yet and the other three Monkees knew they had to include Davy in some way on the album, but weren't sure yet how best to utilize his distinctive style. While the version of this song recorded for *Headquaters* is a lot better than the version here, it does tend to stick out on that record, much like "I'll Spend My Life With You" does. Both of those tracks fit much better alongside the other Boyce & Hart material it was initially recorded with.

The last track recorded by Boyce & Hart for the first record, but held over for the second is **"(I'm Not Your) Steppin' Stone"**. It could be argued that this track belongs more on the next playlist than it does here, since it actually appeared on the second album and not the first. However since only one day separates this song from the last two songs recorded on this playlist, and Boyce and Hart took two whole weeks off before starting the next round of sessions, I have included it in this chapter. The difference between the two playlists is very slight and they could be merged together if one really wanted to, I suppose.

"(I'm Not Your) Steppin' Stone" is another proto-grunge garage-rock number, even more simplistic and furious than "Let's Dance On." It was originally written for and recorded by Paul Revere & The Raiders, and in some ways is not very tailored for the Monkees. However Micky's voice is a lot better than Mark Lindsay's and this track kicks some serious ass. While nominally a simple three chord song, there is a break with just held notes on the organ and a furious beat on the toms that makes the song something special. The backing vocals are perfect. This is exactly the kind of song that Boyce & Hart excelled at and it is a great way to close out this playlist.

BOYCE & HART 2

1.) Valleri 2:34
(written by Tommy Boyce and Bobby Hart)
first released on *Missing Links Vol. II*
August 6th, 1966

2.) Words 3:04
(written by Tommy Boyce and Bobby Hart)
first released on *Missing Links Vol. II*
August 15th, 1966

3.) She 2:37
(written by Tommy Boyce and Bobby Hart)
from *More Of The Monkees*
August 15th, 1966

4.) Ladies Aid Society 2:42
(written by Tommy Boyce and Bobby Hart)
first released on *The Monkees Present*
August 23rd, 1966

5.) Kicking Stones 2:28
(written by Lynn Castle and Wayne Erwin)
first released on *Missing Links Vol. I*
August 23rd, 1966

6.) Mr. Webster 2:55
(written by Tommy Boyce and Bobby Hart)
first released on *Missing Links Vol. II*
September 10th, 1966

7.) Through The Looking Glass 2:36
(written by Tommy Boyce, Bobby Hart and Red Baldwin)
first released on *Missing Links Vol. III*
September 10th, 1966

8.) Teardrop City 2:02
(written by Tommy Boyce and Bobby Hart)
first released on *Instant Replay*
October 26th, 1966

9.) Looking For The Good Times 2:36
(written by Tommy Boyce and Bobby Hart)
first released on *The Monkees Present*
October 26th, 1966

10.) I'll Spend My Life With You 2:30
(written by Tommy Boyce and Bobby Hart)
first released as a bonus track on *More Of The Monkees*
October 26th, 1966

11.) Apples, Beaches, Bananas & Pears 2:16
(written by Tommy Boyce and Bobby Hart)
first released on *Missing Links Vol. II*
October 28th, 1966

12.) Don't Listen To Linda 2:29
(written by Tommy Boyce and Bobby Hart)
first released as a bonus track on *More Of The Monkees*
October 28th, 1966

13.) I Never Thought It Peculiar 2:22
(written by Tommy Boyce and Bobby Hart)
first released on *Changes*
October 26th, 1966

Produced by Tommy Boyce and Bobby Hart

MUSICIANS:
WAYNE ERWIN, GERRY McGEE & LOUIE SHELTON: guitars
LARRY TAYLOR: bass
BILLY LEWIS: drums
GENE ESTES: tambourine, percussion, mallets
ALAN ESTES: timpani, tambourine
BOBBY HART: organ, piano, keyboards
TOMMY BOYCE: acoustic guitar
NORM JEFFRIES: tambourine (on "She"), percussion (on "Words")
EMIL RICHARDS: percussion (on "Ladies Aid Society"), mallets (on "Kicking Stones")
STEVE HUFFSTETER: trumpet (on "Ladies Aid Society" and "Kicking Stones")
DICK HYDE & GILBERT FALCO: trombone (on "Ladies Aid Society" and "Kicking Stones")
BOB JUNG & DON McGINNIS: horns (on "Ladies Aid Society" and "Kicking Stones")
PAUL SUTTER: organ, flute (on "Kicking Stones")
ETHMER ROTEN: flute (on "Words")
MAGGIE AUE: cello (on "Mr. Webster")
NORMAN BENNO: oboe (on "Mr. Webster")
MICHEL RUBINI: tack piano (on "Don't Listen To Linda" and "Through The Looking Glass"),
    harpsichord (on "Mr. Webster")

TOMMY BOYCE, BOBBY HART, RON HICKLIN, WAYNE ERWIN, MICKY DOLENZ, PETER TORK, & DAVY JONES: backing vocals

Recorded 8/6/66 – 10/26/66

If the Monkees had a great unreleased album alá The Beach Boys' *Smile* or Dylan's *The Basement Tapes*, it would be Boyce & Hart's second album for the Monkees. Given the success of the debut album, Tommy Boyce and Bobby Hart must have reasonably assumed they would get the same deal for the second album: producing the entire album aside from a pair of Nesmith outliers. Therefore they went ahead and produced enough material for a follow-up just as soon as they were done with the first album. However, when *More Of The Monkees* came out, only two of Boyce & Hart's tracks ended up on it, and one of those was recorded the day after "The Last Train To Clarksville" making it more of an outtake from the first album than the second.

As a result there ended up being several Boyce & Hart tracks leftover. These were songs that clearly were not produced for the TV show as the lyrics were no longer confined to the usual boy/girl subject matter, but are very plot and story based. Having such narrative lyrics meant that these recordings could not be slotted into episodes of the TV show unless that week's plot involved a teeny tiny gnome or a bank security guard named Mr. Webster. Even so, several of the other less plot-driven lyrics did appear on the show, but weren't available for the audience to purchase in record form. While this is not exactly the best marketing synergy, it did create a demand for these tracks that were still in the vault, but these songs did not languish there too long. Each of the Monkees' albums afterwards, except for the *Head* soundtrack, featured a couple of these tracks either re-recorded or just pasted right in there.

While the general quality of these tracks is pretty high, there are definitely some tracks that are quite derided amongst Monkees' fans (although I will defend a few). However, I think Boyce & Hart's fate on the second album was sealed when Don Kirshner got word back about two random songs from the sessions that don't really paint the best portrait of what was going on: "Teeny Tiny Gnome" and "Ladies Aid Society" both recorded on August 23rd, 1966. These are tunes that do seem to skew to a demographic that might be even younger than one the already pre-pubescent date range that the Powers-That-Be were angling towards.

As for the sound of this never assembled second album, it is pretty much what you'd expect from a sophomore follow-up. The band is still the same guys - only with a lot more horns or strings or whatnot added to the mix, as the bigger budget and greater creative freedom would allow. This may not be as consistent a listen as Boyce & Hart's first playlist, with a much higher ratio of duds. However the highs are much more exciting and

I do find myself listening to this much more than the last playlist. While it does have its share of cringe-worthy moments, it's definitely better than the mish-mash hodge-podge that Don Kirshner assembled for the officially released *More Of The Monkees*.

Right off the bat, Boyce & Hart are trying to shake things up with **"Valleri"**, by having this upbeat rocking tune sung by Davy. Furthermore, while the last album eschewed guitar heroics, this track features some in-your-face flashy flamenco-styled guitar playing from Louis Shelton. While the guitar stylings may seem a bit out of place compared to the rest of the track which is a straight-forward rock song alá "Let's Dance On", both elements are executed so flawlessly and forcefully that it really works as a whole. The track is so jubilant it is no surprise that after it was featured on an episode of the TV show a handful of industrious DJs taped the song to play on the radio eventually creating enough demand that the track was re-recorded (to a much lesser effect) and released on *The Birds, The Bees, & The Monkees*.

On **"Words"** Boyce & Hart finally found a way to use Peter. After his complete vocal absence from the last album, I'm sure Don Kirshner issued an edict that Tork had to be given something on the next album to ensure that the quarter of Monkees fans that considered Pete their favorite would also plunk down their hard-earned cash for the record. It had nothing to do with whether or not Don Kirshner or anyone else thought Peter's voice was any good. Boyce & Hart answered this challenge by giving him only half of a lead vocal so that not too much pressure was put on his weak pipes. His flat spooky answering vocals work really well for this song (both for this version and the one re-done for *Pisces, Aquarius, Capricorn, & Jones, Ltd.*) Overall, this is a far more psychedelic sounding mid-tempo song that was neither the proto-grunge of their rock songs nor the sappy ballads that most of the first album vacillated between.

"She", however, fits exactly within the hard-edge template of such songs as "(I'm Not Your) Steppin' Stone". However they are refining their formula and making it even stronger. "She" is even darker and angrier than their previous rock tunes. The main riff is pretty much two notes making this song seem almost punk. The slightly slower tempo makes the track even more menacing, and the fact that the object of the song is deliberately never named adds to the general disdain and hurt the narrator feels. The organ solo is merely a recapitulation of the vocal melody, but it works. Overall this first three songs show a much stronger, heavier sound from Boyce & Hart for the Monkees on this playlist, but this wasn't all they had up their sleeves.

"Ladies Aid Society" is frequently picked by Monkees fans as one of the weakest tracks in the entire catalogue. Maybe because the album this finally appeared on, *The Monkees Present*, is one of the first I bought and loved, I have a soft-spot in my heart for this song. Granted it's a stilted and forced attempt to re-create the spontaneous fun of "Gonna Buy Me A Dog" and fill the novelty-song slot on the record.

The use of falsetto is a hackneyed way of pretending to sound female that really isn't funny for anyone over the age of twelve. The vague anti-establishment sentiment of lyrics has not held up very well. In the 60s it was pretty popular to rail against the so-called "straights" or "squares" for being responsible for all of the evils in the world without presenting any real logic or reasoning behind it. All that aside, this song is a lot of fun, especially if you stay with the version on *The Monkees Present* and not the mono version that ended up as bonus track on the deluxe re-issue of *More Of The Monkees*. That version adds almost an entire minute to length with unnecessary sound effects and repeats of the chorus. The faux-salvation army band playing in the chorus is great touch, and Davy tries his best to sell it as sweetly as possible while really getting into the campiness of the falsetto bits.

The next song, **"Kicking Stones"** (also known as "Teeny Tiny Gnome") also tries to undermine everything that the first three tracks established. Again, this track is supposed to be funny, but fails. The lyrics are an "Alice In Wonderland" pastiche with weird events culminating in no sort of drama, tension or meaning. Significantly, this song was not written by Boyce & Hart, but by sessions guitarist, Wayne Erwin with words by Lynn Castle who was reportedly Boyce & Hart's hairdresser. The music is a sort-of charming shuffle but not terribly memorable. The quote-unquote magic flute solo sounds neither musical nor fantastical. It just sounds like an organ badly recorded and distorted (which I think is what it actually was). This is one of the weakest tracks on the playlist, and not surprisingly was one of the two songs here that was not released in some form during the Monkees original nine album run.

The next song also has a plot-driven story, only its lyrics that works much better. **"Mr. Webster"** conveys that sort of malaise at the stuffed-shirt society that "Ladies Aid Society" and "Pleasant Valley Sunday" are going for, but does it much better by keeping the story more specific and less of a broad indictment of the entire establishment. The lyrics tell the story of a bank guard who does a good job of protecting the bank's assets but still gets screwed by the man when it comes time for raises. So what does the hapless bank guard do? He uses his knowledge of the workings of the bank to rob them blind while everyone's away at his retirement party.

The arrangement, with its harpsichords and oboes, starts and stops and gives this otherwise mundane and small story and the grandeur of epic, or at least the import of a morality tale. The version of this song on *Headquarters* makes the story a little smaller and more relatable, but this version is a lot more understated and restrained than it could've been. Also ot note, this is the third song in a row that has nothing to do with boy-girl romantic relationships. While the last playlist was exclusively focused on that subject, Boyce & Hart have now decided that it was important to try and tackle different subject matter this time around.

"Through The Looking Glass" however is another love song. Or at least it is a "girl, you gotta shape up" song. Unfortunately it is not a companion piece to the Lewis Carroll-styled "Kicking Stones." It is not one of the more memorable songs on this collection, being chugging without rocking and not having anything super-catchy. At least this early version is pretty feels bright and strummy as opposed to the version that was later recorded for *The Birds, The Bees, & The Monkees* but was used to open *Instant Replay*. That version is drags and comes across as a little self-important and pretentious with the strings and horns on it.

But when comparing the original to the version on *Instant Replay*, **"Tear Drop City"** actually is better on the latter album. Only instead of being a re-recording, it is the exact same song only with the tape sped up a lot. At the original tempo it was recorded at, the song comes off as an unremarkable blues-y rock number. Sped-up though, it feels a lot more alive and interesting. Plus you get through it faster. The song is one of Boyce & Hart's first attempts to duplicate the success of "Last Train To Clarksville". Only it was not as good; the riff is not as memorable and the lyrics are not as clever. When it was released as a single it did not do nearly as well in the charts as "Clarksville", and is now generally a forgotten song in the Monkees' oeuvre. As usual, the faster version of a Monkees' song – (especially one by Boyce & Hart) is the better version.

Speaking of fast songs, here's another great one: **"Looking For The Good Times"**. Like "Valleri", Boyce & Hart are branching out and giving more up-tempo songs for Davy to sing. Louis Shelton is given another showcase to demonstrate his fluidity with the guitar. Again my affection for this tune may be influenced by the fact that it was included on *The Monkees Present*. While I still like this song, I will admit that it not really as good of a song as "Valleri."

Not only have Boyce & Hart been pretty good about giving Davy the type of rockers that Micky usually gets to sing; here they give Micky a chance to sing on this kind of music hall number **"I'll Spend My Life With You"**. Again it's hard not imagine tap-dancing to this song. This feels like the kind of song that Boyce & Hart would include trying please the grandparents of whatever teenage girl bought this record. Micky does add a wistful air to the vocals that make this track a lot less cloying than it would've been in Davy's hands. For no good reason this is one of the tunes that the Monkees redid for *Headquarters* once they took control of their musical destiny. While that version is superior in the weird way that Mike's amateur-ish pedal steel guitar is integrated into the mix, the original version does gives a better idea of types of things that Boyce & Hart could do with the Monkees as well as the chances they were starting to take with this second set of sessions.

"Apples, Peaches, Bananas, & Pears" is another attempt by Boyce & Hart to recapture the lightning-in-a-bottle that was "Last Train To Clarksville". Again it has their trademark non-solo solo in the middle. While this is a much more successful rewrite in terms of the music than "Tear Drop City", this song is horribly dragged down by its lyrics. It's not that the lyrics don't make sense, I just can't understand why they're being sung. Is the protagonist so poor that the only gifts he can offer his beloved are fruit? Or he is so stupid that he thinks that this is what she really wants? Or does she not have the ability to buy these fruit for herself for some reason? Is it supposed to sarcastic, and that she is only worth these things? Or is Micky supposed to literally be a monkey here, so that wooing a potential mate with fruit would actually seem impressive? I have no idea. There's nothing in the lyrics that shows that the protagonist knows what a pitiful offer he is making. Other than that, it is a pretty good track. I think the lyrical conceit is so whacked-out that this is the reason that "Apples, Peaches, Bananas, & Pears" is the only other song here that wasn't released on one of the original Monkees' albums.

While the playlist started strong, things are starting to get bad. "I'll Spend My Life With You" was not Boyce & Hart's only Herman's Hermits-styled track here. **"Don't Listen To Linda"** lays it on even thicker and has Davy hamming it up endlessly on the vocals. There's even a faux-kazoo clarinet solo in the song. As bad as this gets, this song was made even worse when it was given the "Through The Looking Glass" treatment (recorded for *The Birds, The Bees, & The Monkees* but released on *Instant Replay*). Where the initial "Don't Listen To Linda" was an annoying trifle the re-make is stretched out into a portentous sermon layered with syrupy orchestration and then slowed to a somber crawl. No song deserves that sort of treatment - not even "Don't Listen To Linda."

The last track on this playlist is definitely better, but **"I Never Thought It Peculiar"** is still in the same vein as "I'll Spend My Life With You" and "Don't Listen To Linda". It's another soft-shoe, straw hat, and cane number. The best parts of the song is where it goes from 4/4 to waltz time without dropping a beat or breaking a sweat. The only other part of the song that puts it ahead of the others is the somewhat out-of-place guitar solo that may have been their attempt to ape Hendrix or the popular "heavy" rock sound of 1969. This overdub was apparently added nearly three years after the rest of the track was finished, but to my ears feels like a necessary part of the song that had always been planned on and not a horrendous attempt to try and update the song for the latest fads and trends.

While this is the last we'd hear from Boyce & Hart on the Monkees for a while, they wouldn't be gone from the project they helped start forever. However, by the time the Monkees did come crawling back things would be very different.

BOYCE & HART 3

1.) Me Without You
(written by Tommy Boyce and Bobby Hart)
first released on *Instant Replay*
December 26th, 1967

2.) P. O. Box 9847
(written by Tommy Boyce and Bobby Hart)
first released on *The Birds, The Bees, & The Monkees*
December 26th, 1967

3.) My Storybook Of You
(written by Tommy Boyce and Bobby Hart)
first released on *Missing Links Vol. 1*
May 3rd, 1969

REMAKES RECORDED THESE SESSIONS:
Valleri (from "Boyce & Hart 2" released on *The Birds, The Bees, & The Monkees*)
Don't Listen To Linda (from "Boyce & Hart 2" released on *Instant Replay*)
Through The Looking Glass (from "Boyce & Hart 2" released on *Instant Replay*)

Produced by Tommy Boyce and Bobby Hart

MUSICIANS:
GERRY McGEE & LOUIE SHELTON: guitar
JOE OSBORN: bass
BILLY LEWIS: drums
BOBBY HART: keyboards
JOHN GALLIE: piano (on "My Storybook Of You")
LARRY KNETCHEL: tack piano (on "My Storybook Of You")
VICTOR ARNO & JACK PEPPER: violin (on "P.O. Box 9847")
BILL KURSACH, JEROME RESLER, RALPH SCHAEFFER, SIDNEY SHARP, & SHARI
    ZIPPERT: violin (on "My Storybook Of You")
PHILIP GOLDBERG: viola (on "P.O. Box 9847")

JESSE EHRLICH: cello (on "My Storybook Of You")
RAYMOND KELLEY: cello (on "P.O. Box 9847")
JAY MIGLIORI: sax (on "My Storybook Of You")
JULES CHAIKIN & OLIVER MITCHELL: trumpet (on "My Storybook Of You")
DICK NASH: trombone (on "My Storybook Of You")

recorded 12/26/67 and 5/3/69

Boyce & Hart were accidental casualties of the foursome's palace revolt against Don Kirschner. But once the novelty of producing their own records wore off, The Monkees were once again open to using outside musicians and (uncredited) producers. Naturally, one of the first people they turned to were Boyce & Hart. One of the first things the Monkees needed Boyce & Hart to do was re-record "Valleri", because there was a great demand for this song thanks to it being placed on the TV show. However, the original version couldn't be released because the new rule of law stated that all songs had to be credited as "produced by the Monkees". So Boyce & Hart re-recorded this song along with "Don't Listen To Linda" and "Through The Looking Glass" anonymously. They also came in and recorded a couple of new songs. Most of these didn't get released at the time either, but continued to dribble out on subsequent albums. I'm not sure why these later versions were the ones which originally saw the light of day as none of these productions could hold a candle to the original crop of tunes recorded in 1966.

The new songs that Boyce & Hart did at this point show their disinterest in the project. They may have felt slighted by the way they were treated by the Monkees organization, but were willing to do this as their own career as a performing duo had stalled. They do not seem nearly as interested or involved in these songs as they were when they thought of the Monkees as their pet project. Also, writing for the Monkees was by this point no longer seen as the springboard to bigger and better things, but just another job for a professional songwriting and producing team. They did seem content at this period just to re-record stuff they had already written far more than they were interested in pushing themselves to write new material.

Part of the problem with this new batch of recordings is that it is no longer the Candy Store Prophets playing. Wayne Erwin, the only non-session guitarist from the other playlists, is gone and Larry Taylor has been replaced by studio bassist Joe Osborn. So this doesn't have the cohesive lived-in feel that the earlier tracks did. Boyce & Hart also seem to want to show off as mature sophisticated producers at this point, slowing down all the tempos till they drag and slathering on goopy strings and horns to try and appeal to a more mature adult audience. Mature and adult is not Boyce & Hart's strong suit. "Through The Looking Glass" and "Don't Listen To Linda" are rendered nearly unlistenable compared to the older versions.

Fortunately, the original version of "Valleri" was already widely known so that they couldn't slow down and rearrange that one too much. They did add horns though which did lessen the overall dynamic punch of the song by making it sound too forced.

Even on these newly written songs, they weren't trying very hard. While Boyce & Hart have certainly been heavily influenced before, the track **"Me Without You"** is almost direct rip-ff of the Beatles' "Your Mother Should Know" (which isn't one of the Beatles' better songs to begin with). You can easily sing the words to the Beatles song over this. Again, it's got a kind of music hall feel, with Davy singing lead, of course. Not only does it sound like the same song, but the arrangements are unnervingly similar as well, with clarinets to fore. About all Boyce & Hart add to this rip-off is a lead guitar solo that the Beatles original is missing. Still it feels very lazy and disinterested for Boyce & Hart.

"P.O. Box 9847" comes off a lot better. While it is homage to the more psychedelic sound of the time, it is not nearly as blatantly lifted from anyone single source. Furthermore, the conceit of song is interesting lyrically. We get to know more and more about the desires and insecurities of the protagonist by listening to each discarded draft he has written for a personal ad. The odd hammered dulcimer and frantic strings are kind of cool, but can also a little distracting. This is not nearly as successful an attempt at capturing the zeitgeist of the time as "The Porpoise Song." It certainly sounds like a product of its time, but compared to the other tunes Boyce & Hart were doing at the time, it is easily their best.

After finishing their work on these two new songs and three re-recordings in late 1967, Boyce & Hart left the Monkees' project again, only to be called in to try and save the day one last time in May of 1969. And what one track did they bring to try and revive the Monkees' declining fortunes and to close out their stint with the band that they arguably helped birth? A slow mawkish ballad for Davy, **"My Storybook Of You"**. It is trite syrupy treacle. Clearly Boyce & Hart had given up on trying to recapture their now maturing original audience and decided to aim for their little sisters who were now young kids just starting to get into pop music. The storybook theme and the mushy romantic sentiment of lyrics seem coldly calculated to melt the hearts of 11-year-olds. Sadly, it just comes off as a little embarrassing and was, understandably, unreleased at the time.

This was an unfortunate note for them to end their careers with the Monkees on... unless you count 1976's explanatorily titled *Dolenz, Jones, Boyce, & Hart*. I almost included that album as it actually sounds closer to a Monkees reunion album than 1987's *Pool It!* or 1996's *Justus* but decided to pass because it was not officially released under the Monkees' name.

GERRY GOFFIN & CAROLE KING

1.) I Don't Think You Know Me 2:20
(written by Gerry Goffin and Carole King)
first released as a bonus track on *More Of The Monkees*
October 13th, 1966

2.) Sometime In The Morning 2:31
(written by Gerry Goffin and Carole King)
from *More Of The Monkees*
October 13th, 1966

3.) The Porpoise Song 2:37
(written by Gerry Goffin and Carole King)
from the soundtrack to *Head*
February 26th, 1968

4.) Look Down 2:52
(written by Carole King and Toni Stern)
first released on *Missing Links Vol. III*
April 6th, 1968

5.) As We Roll Along 3:46
(written by Carole King and Toni Stern)
from the soundtrack to *Head*
May 30th, 1968

UNFINISHED SONGS FROM THE 1968 SESSIONS:
Carlisle Wheeling (written by Michael Nesmith)
Dear Marm (written by Gerry Goffin and Carole King)

Produced by Carole King & Gerry Goffin

MUSICIANS for the 1966 tracks:
TOMMY TEDESCO, AL CASEY & DENNIS BUDIMIR: guitar

LARRY KNETCHEL: bass
MICHEL RUBINI: piano
HAL BLAINE: drums
KEN WATSON: percussion
JULES CHAIKIN & ANTHONY TERRAN: trumpet
LEWIS McCREARY: trombone
JIM HORN & JAY MIGLIORI: sax

MUSICIANS for the 1968 tracks:
KEN BLOOM, RY COODER, CAROLE KING, DANNY
    KORTCHMAR, TONY McCASHEN & NEIL YOUNG: guitar
DOUG LUBAHN, HARVEY NEWMARK, & LARRY KNETCHEL:
    bass
MICHAEL NEY, JOHN RAINES, EARL PALMER, & HAL BLAINE:
    drums
LEON RUSSELL, RALPH SCHUCKETT, & MICHAEL RUBINI: piano
DENNIS BUDIMIR, AL CASEY, & TOMMY TEDESCO: guitar (on
    "Look Down")
KEN WATSON: percussion
GREGORY BEMKO, DAVID FILERMAN, JAN KELLEY, & JACQUELINE LUSTGARTEN:
    cello
MAX BENNETT, CLYDE HOGGAN, JIM HUGHART & JERRY SCHEFF: double bass
BILL HINSHAW & JULES JACOB: brass and woodwind
JULES CHAIKIN & TONY TERRAN: trumpet
LEW McCREARY: trombone

recorded 10/13/14 and 2/26/68 - 5/30/68

The difference between the two pre-"Kirshner exile" songs and the two post-Kirshner tracks is a microcosm of the entire sea change that had occurred within the Monkees as a musical entity. The 1966 tracks are light poppy songs concerned with boy/girl relationships, while the 1968 track are fantastical *Sgt. Pepper*-wannabe songs with trippy psychedelic lyrics. While Carole King's story is predicated on the fact she was writing monster hits for others while her own voice was being left unheard, the tunes she wrote for the Monkees generally were not the kind of stuff she would be singing herself, with possible exception of "Pleasant Valley Sunday." While she and her partner Gerry Goffin got to write a lot of material for the other producers to use for the Monkees, they were occasionally granted the opportunity to try and produce for the Monkees themselves.

It's doubtful that Goffin & King chose Peter Tork to sing lead on **"I Don't Think You Know Me At All"** because of his voice. More likely, they thought it was a good way to ensure that the song made it on to the album since Don Kirshner had decreed that Peter should have one lead vocal on the second album regardless of how badly he sang. This ploy didn't work and this song was not released during the original run of the Monkees. This does mean there are versions of this song now available sung by everyone in the band except for Davy. Of all of them, Peter's singing is the one that takes the most getting used to, to put it charitably. On the other hand, unlike the other versions produced by Mike, this one is probably closer to the commercial pop that Goffin & King had in mind when they wrote it. And while Peter's voice is not great, he does okay -- it just wasn't good fit for his image at the time which was more in line with the goofy dumbbell from the TV show than the earnest hippie that he was in real life.

Goffin & King's other production from the time however did manage to find a slot on Don Kirshner's *More Of The Monkees*. Like "I Don't Think You Know Me At All", **"Sometime In The Morning"** is a fairly standard straight-ahead pop-rock production of its time. It is a slightly slow ballad-y tune. They at least had Micky and not Davy singing it, turning in a fine vocal performance although the lyrics are fairly bland and the instrumentation and arrangement sounds a little muddy with nothing able to really stand out.

During the time that the Monkees had taken over their music and then gotten bored and given it back to professionals like Goffin & King, popular music had completely changed. The Monkees were no longer the fresh-faced young innocents from your TV screen; the show had come and gone by this point and now they were ready to make their own bitter, cynical, realistic cinematic expose on the life of plastic pop phenomenon. It's kind of odd that at this juncture they invited Goffin & King, who used to be seen as Kirshner lackeys, to pen and produce some of the more important tracks for their movie, *Head*. While the Monkees took a lot of heat at the time for not being a real band, just playing at making music, when the Beatles invaded the Monkees turf by making *Magical Mystery Tour* the same criticism has not hurled back at them. While the TV show was modeled on *A Hard Day's Night*, *Magical Mystery Tour* is the closest analog to the Monkees' film *Head*, and clearly you can tell which one was made by seasoned veterans of the film set and which was made by the naive amateurs.

While Goffin & King's 1966 productions were clearly modeled on the safe pop of its day, **"The Porpoise Song"** is obviously attempting to ape the more adventurous psychedelic sound of the post-*Sgt. Pepper*, summer-of-love era. However, Goffin & King had also gotten a lot more experience and maturity under their belt, so while this is still a cynical commercial ploy to cash-in on the latest fad, "The Porpoise Song" is much better than Goffin & King's previous work for the Monkees. The cellos recall "I Am The Walrus" while the lyrics are pure gibberish attempting to sound meaningful. Still it sounds really cool and holds up to the test of time unlike a lot of similar material recorded at the time. It is also one of the few songs where Micky & Davy share the lead vocals, although Micky is carrying the lion's share here.

While "The Porpoise Song" does a great job of mimicking the psycho-jello sounds of the time, **"Look Down"** is an attempt to do the soul, R&B type of thing that Motown was still having hits with. While the music is a perfectly admirable copy of the style and the lyrics are simple but functional, the track is undone a bit by the choice of Davy as the lead singer. Davy Jones is one of the whitest singers around, and while he does his best here, this just isn't his cup of tea. Especially when, toward the end, Davy yells out "Hold on, I'm coming!" We're reminded just how much he isn't Sam and/or Dave. Maybe if Goffin & King had gotten Micky to sing "Look Down" it would've worked. While it isn't bad, there's a reason this song didn't come out during the Monkees' original run. Still it's always a good thing to hear Davy sing something other than another slow sappy romantic ballad.

Much more successful is another faux-psychedelic song, **"As We Roll Along"**. This song, while not as famous as its cousin, "The Porpoise Song" may be even better. Micky turns in a stellar vocal performance, gliding over the trick time signature of 5/4 with grace and ease. The track is light and breezy, but still with a lot going on. The flutes are nice; and while the strange meter should've made the song angular and clunky, it floats by so gently you don't even notice the odd time signature at first. I'm not quite sure why there are so many guitar superstars just strumming along acoustically on this song, but it works. There are not a lot of metrically complex songs like this in the Monkees' catalog ("My Share Of The Sidewalk" and "Love Is Only Sleeping" are about it) and since they were usually relying on studio musicians they certainly could've tried more intricate stuff like this more often. Unlike Boyce & Hart, Goffin & King were never very reliant on the Monkees for their income and so they didn't do a lot of production work for them, but if they had done more stuff like "As We Roll Along" it would've been alright by me.

NEIL SEDAKA & CAROLE BAYER

1.) When Love Comes Knockin' (At Your Door) 1:48
(written by Neil Sedaka & Carole Bayer)
from *More Of The Monkees*
November 23rd, 1966

2.) The Girl I Left Behind Me 2:46
(written by Neil Sedaka & Carole Bayer)
first released on *Instant Replay*
November 23rd, 1966

Produced by Neil Sedaka & Carole Bayer

MUSICIANS:
AL GAFA, WILLARD SUYKER & DON THOMAS: guitar
NEIL SEDAKA: keyboards
RUSS SAVAKUS: bass
HERB LOVELLE: drums
JULIUS SCHACHTER & LEO KAHN: violin (on "The Girl I Left Behind Me")
MAURICE BIALKIN: cello (on "The Girl I Left Behind Me")

recorded 11/23/66

The arrival of the Beatles on the international stage was not necessarily good news for everyone. Professional songwriters everywhere must've worried for their jobs as it was now expected that bands also write their own material. Part of the reason that Don Kirshner was able to get the Monkees such good stuff was that the demand for these professional Brill Building songwriters had dried up in the wake of Beatlemania. Of course, a number of these songwriters used the clout that writing for the Monkees gave them as a springboard to performing careers of their own; some successfully (like Carole King and Neil Diamond) and others less so (Boyce

& Hart). Even Neil Sedaka's partner here, Carole Bayer, would eventually become something bigger after her involvement here.

Neil Sedaka on the other hand has taking the reverse career route. Having once been a singer of such hits as "Calendar Girl" and "Breaking Up Is Hard To Do", Neil Sedaka now was having troubles as a recording artist, so he went into being a behind-the-scenes songwriter and producer. Of course Neil Sedaka was still well-known enough for Don Kirshner to name-drop him on the liner notes of the second album as if to say: "look at all the impressive people I got to work for me!"

The schlock that Neil Sedaka came up with for the Monkees is some of the worst that ever got attached to their name. This is the stuff that Don Kirshner loved; thoroughly calculated to melt the young hearts of teen girls everywhere, and needless to say they both feature Davy Jones. While something like "Sometime In The Morning" sounds deliberately calculated, it doesn't have the disdain for its young audience that seems to drip from these two tracks.

Of the two songs **"When Love Comes Knockin' (At Your Door)"** fares better as it is more up-tempo. The lyrics, in addition to being pure cheese, seemed designed to force Davy to emphasis his English accent even more than ever. The use of the second person seems particularly crass in winning over the less sophisticated listener. Still it's poppy and you can snap your fingers to it. Not an earworm by any stretch, but still catchy. It's completely harmless album filler, and there's nothing wrong with that. Still not only could the Monkees do so much better they were doing so much better at this time and that stuff wasn't getting. The best thing you can say about this song is that it is really short, being under two minutes.

The next track is even worse. **"The Girl I Left Behind Me"** is so sweetly saccharine it could cause a listener to get diabetes. For a song whose lyrics are theoretically about regret there is nothing sad or angry or angst-ridden about this music. Of course this is the kind of thing that showcases the image of Davy that he was always foisting upon the public. When this track was left initially unreleased, it is not surprise that Davy re-recorded it, not once but twice. Still when this song finally did see the light of day, it was this version and not one of Davy's that was released on *Instant Replay*. While Neil Sedaka's production may have been pure elevator Muzak at least he was a master at it as opposed to Davy Jones. Luckily Neil Sedaka did not do any more production for the Monkees after the ousting of Kirshner. Still it is unimaginable that of all the great stuff recorded and left behind by the Monkees, both of Neil's songs were released commercially.

JEFF BARRY 1

1.)   Hold On Girl 2:44*
(written by Jack Keller, Ben Raleigh and Billy Carr)
from *More Of The Monkees*
October 14th, 1966

2.)   Your Auntie Grizelda 2:27*
(written by Jack Keller and Diane Hildebrand)
from *More Of The Monkees*
October 14th, 1966

3.)   Look Out (Here Comes Tomorrow) 2:14
(written by Neil Diamond)
from *More Of The Monkees*
October 15th, 1966

4.)   I'm A Believer 2:44
(written by Neil Diamond)
from *More Of The Monkees*
October 15th, 1966

5.)   Laugh 2:26
(written by Hank Medress, Phil Margo, Mitchell Margo and Jay Siegal)
from *More Of The Monkees*
October 28th, 1966

6.)   I'll Be Back Up On My Feet 2:39
(written by Sandy Linzer and Denny Randell)
first released on *Missing Links Vol. II*
October 28th, 1966

7.)   The Day We Fall In Love 2:22
(written by Sandy Linzer and Denny Randell)
from *More Of The Monkees*
October 28th, 1966

Produced by Jeff Barry, except
*Produced by Jeff Barry and Jack Keller

MUSICIANS:
AL CASEY & CAROLE KAYE: guitar
DON RANDI & MICHEL RUBINI: keyboards
RAY POHLMAN: bass
HAL BLAINE: drums
FRANK CAPP & JULIIUS WECHTER: percussion
LOUIS HABER, IRVING SPICE & LOUIS STONE: violin (on "The Day We Fall In Love")
DAVID SACKSON & MURRAY SANDRY: viola (on "The Day We Fall In Love")
SEYMOUR BARAB: cello (on "The Day We Fall In Love")
ARTIE BUTLER: string arrangement (on "The Day We Fall In Love")
NEIL DIAMOND: acoustic guitar (on "Look Out (Here Comes Tomorrow)" and "I'm A Believer")
BUDDY SALZMAN: drums (on "Look Out (Here Comes Tomorrow)" and "I'm A Believer")

recorded 10/14/66 - 10/28/66

While Don Kirshner included two tracks apiece from Michael Nesmith and Boyce & Hart and one each from Neil Sedaka and Goffin & King, six of the twelve tracks on *More Of The Monkees* was produced by Don Kirshner's personal favorite producer, Jeff Barry. While Boyce & Hart's first album may have initially created what The Monkees were supposed to sound like, it is Jeff Barry's production that has most popular and well known Monkees' sound. It is certainly the most commercial and poppy sound the Monkees ever had, but it also the sound that is most susceptible to the common criticisms of the Monkees being plastic and shallow. However, Jeff Barry's songs are the ones which most of the general public and even casual Monkees fans think of when they think of the Monkees.

The difference between the two early "Monkees don't play their own instruments" factions is best demonstrated by the song **"Hold On Girl"**. The song was written by Jack Keller amongst others. Jack Keller was dispatched by Don Kirshner to co-produce both Boyce & Hart and Jeff Barry's first few sessions just to make sure they were delivering product that Don Kirshner would like. Boyce & Hart's version wasn't made available until the compilation *Missing Links Vol. II* came out in 1990 and is one of the few songs they produced that they didn't write. It is not a great song, but works pretty well as fun up-tempo pop song with driving hand claps and a goofy harpsichord and drum riff.

Boyce & Hart's production of this song however is slowed down just enough to get boring. Their version is still using the harpsichord, only here to give the whole song a pretentious faux-classical feel accentuated by the use of the timpani. Also, without the drums on the riff the song doesn't rev up but rather comes to an awkward stop each time that part comes up. This is one of the only times where I would find a Jeff Barry production preferable to a Boyce & Hart. Even odder is the fact that Don Kirshner and I agree on this track as he put Jeff Barry's version on the released album.

While Davy was his personal favorite, Don Kirshner wanted to make sure that all the Monkees appeared on their second album, if just to ensure that all the Monkees' fan-girls bought the album. So Kirshner had to find a way to get Peter Tork's vocals (but not playing) somewhere on *More Of The Monkees*. Each of Don's producers tried different ways to tailor a song for Peter's unique vocal talents. Boyce & Hart tried to avoid having to really use him by getting him only sing half of "Words." Goffin & King tried playing to Peter's real life personality and ignoring his vocal limitations on "I Don't Think You Know Me At All." Jeff Barry won the prize however by going with a song that fit more with Peter's character on the TV show. While it should be an embarrassing comedy number, **"Your Auntie Grizelda"** works much better in the novelty "Ringo" slot than "Ladies Aid Society" does.

It really shouldn't work. It features the same bland backing that all of Jeff Barry's work had musically and the lyrics are your typical "don't trust anyone over 30" tripe that generally doesn't age very well. What really sells the song is Peter's vocals. While his singing may be a bit unorthodox, this song really fits well with his charming goofball persona and Tork really sells it. He even makes the "mouth noise solo" work, when it would've just been painful if attempted by any of the other Monkees. To the general public, this is the only Peter-sung song the Monkees did, and Peter would have only one more solo lead vocal released during the entire original album run.

While "Your Auntie Grizelda" worked, Jeff Barry did try to get Peter on the album again in another comedy role by having him do quote-unquote wacky comedy bits during parts of **"Look Out (Here Comes Tomorrow)"**. While it a clever conceit, it just distracts from the song it was tacked onto and was wisely removed before the song was released. This is one of the first Neil Diamond songs that Monkees recorded. Not surprisingly all of the Neil Diamond tunes they did were produced by Jeff Barry. While it is terribly commercial it really doesn't fit the Monkees very well and sounds more like a Neil Diamond song.

This is perfectly fine tune, but has nothing to really recommend it. It's kind of hard to sympathize with a guy who has two girls who are into him but aren't as willing to share as the protagonist clearly wants. It's nice that they gave an upbeat song to Davy to sing, although it is starting to become obvious that both Don Kirshner and Jeff Barry see Davy as the main vocalist in the Monkees with the other three just being thrown the occasional bone.

The next Jeff Barry production is another Neil Diamond tune, **"I'm A**

Believer". This song is at least better than "Look Out (Here Comes Tomorrow)" if only because Micky's voice is better suited to this material than Davy's. While it is a solidly constructed pop-song it isn't nearly half as good as "Last Train To Clarksville". I have resigned myself to seeing this song in any Monkees live setlist or compilation, but personally I could do without it. It is very catchy and it is easy to see why it became a hit. However, why this song has endured only to be brought to further prominence by Smashmouth and *Shrek* is beyond my comprehension. Most Monkees albums have at least one or two album tracks that are at least as good as this if not better. It is not even their best hit with the word "believer" in the title.

While "Your Auntie Grizelda" should've been the only quote-unquote funny song on the album, somehow we also get the inappropriately titled **"Laugh"**. It is a song about the importance of humor where all the attempts at humor fall flat. It almost reminds me of Alanis Morissette's song "Ironic" that doesn't actually manage to give a single accurate example of irony. Maybe if Peter had sung this one too it would've worked better. The backing musical track is pretty standard and unengaging - most notably the bass is not offbeat at all, despite the lyrics claiming it is several times. The backing vocals of "ho ha ha ha" are dreadful. Despite the alleged levity of the lyrics, whole song feels rather grim. Sadly, this is not the worst song that Jeff Barry came up with for this playlist.

Next up we have **"I'll Be Back Up On My Feet"**, an chugging little number with Micky on vocals. Despite being featured on the TV show and being one of the best tracks in this set, this is the only song that wasn't released at the time on the second album, although it was re-recorded by Lester Sill for *The Birds, The Bees, & The Monkees*. While that version has some weird cool percussion thing called the quica, the original is better. Not a great song, but still a perfectly fine album filler track. There is certainly nothing wrong with it, unlike the next song.

Words cannot fully describe the sentimental dreck that is **"The Day We Fall In Love"** a song that is not sung by Davy, but rather is spoken. It was horribly dated when it was released and time has only been worse to it. You could theoretically sing rather than speak these words to the backing track and it would be 100 times better, while still being pretty horrible. As it is, it falls somewhere between Richard Harris and William Shatner in terms of pretentious spoken-word poetry. As serious as it tries to be, it never comes close to feeling sincere or heartfelt. It doesn't even feel like a creepy old man trying to woo his underage audience, it's too cynical for that. This is just pure commercial pabulum - and while it is the nadir of Jeff Barry's work for this playlist, it is an apt representative of the whole sound and feel of this batch of songs.

JEFF BARRY 2

1.) Love To Love 2:30
(written by Neil Diamond)
first released on *Missing Links Vol. III* and *Good Times!*
January 21st, 1967

2.) You Can't Tie A Mustang Down 2:58
(written by Jeff Barry)
first released as a bonus track on *Headquarters*
January 21st, 1967

3.) 99 Pounds 2:12
(written by Jeff Barry)
from *Changes*
January 21st, 1967

4.) A Little Bit Me, A Little Bit You 2:51
(written by Neil Diamond)
released as a non-album single
January 21st, 1967

5.) She Hangs Out 2:36
(written by Jeff Barry)
first released on *Missing Links Vol. III*
January 21st, 1967

6.) Gotta Give It Time
(written by Jeff Barry and Joey Levine)
from *Good Times!*
January 21st, 1967

7.) If I Learned To Play The Violin 2:48
(written by Joey Levine and Artie Resnick)
first released as a bonus track on *Headquarters*
January 26th, 1967

UNFINISHED SONGS FROM THESE SESSIONS:

Poor Little Me (written by Jeff Barry and Andy Kim)

Black And Blue (written by Neil Diamond, Jerry Lieber, and Mike Stoller)

Eve Of My Sorrow (written by Jeff Barry, Joey Levine, Jerry Lieber, and Mike Stoller)

The Love You Got Inside (written by Jeff Barry, Andy Kim, Jerry Lieber, and Mike Stoller)

Produced by Jeff Barry

MUSICIANS:

AL GORGONI, HUGH McCRACKEN & DON THOMAS: guitar

STAN FREE: clavinet

ARTIE BUTLER: organ

LOU MAURO: bass

HERB LOVELLE: drums

TOM CERONE: tambourine

JAMES TYRELL: bass (on "If I Learned To Play The Violin")

recorded 1/21/67 - 1/26/67

This definitely sounds like Kirshner and Jeff Barry trying to capitalize on the success of "I'm A Believer" as quickly as they can. So once again there are fast-paced Neil Diamond tunes and knockoffs with plenty of Farfisa organ. The one thing that they couldn't replicate though was Micky Dolenz's vocals. Micky was standing firm with Peter and Mike in boycotting anything Kirshner-related. However, being stuck with Davy probably pleased Don Kirshner and Jeff Barry more than it irked them. Since timing was everything here and they wanted to strike while the iron was hot, they went ahead and recorded all of these songs with Davy singing rather than waiting to see how this labor dispute straightened itself out. What neither one probably realized at the time was that this was going to be the last thing that Don Kirshner ever really did with the Monkees.

Unintentionally, the quick time-frame in which this was recorded gives the songs more of a loose, live band feel to them than the previous set of Jeff Barry productions. Most of these songs were recorded in one day. The only really slow ballad of the bunch is "If I Learned To Play The Violin" which was also the only song that wasn't recorded on the first day. While not a great set of tracks, this imposition actually caused Jeff Barry to step up his game a notch.

"Love To Love" is far more the dark, somber Neil Diamond of "Solitary Man" than the fun Neil Diamond of "Cherry Cherry". The sound is pretty well-established off the bat; heavy organ use and strumming acoustic guitars. The riff sounds reminiscent of "Girl You'll Be A Woman Soon." The production here is better than the version that Neil himself recorded with the unnecessary horns on it. Davy however does not have the resignation and hurt in his voice that Neil does. Still it's a pretty good starter to this set.

"You Can't Tie A Mustang Down" although written by Jeff Barry, sounds a lot closer to "I'm A Believer" than "Love To Love" does. The music is rollicking enough, and the opening guitar riff starts things off well. The lyrics are more of the "I Wanna Be Free" type. It's a plea from a commitment-phobic narrator to the object of his affection that he should be allowed to have his cake and eat it too, because it's not in the singer's nature to be monogamous. Or even particularly honest, since he appears to be making vows of some sort through his actions, but they are simply being misinterpreted by the woman in question. It's kind of creepy, but the real issue raised by the lyrics is; does anyone think there is any difference between tying something down and tying something up.

Luckily **"99 Pounds"** is far less misogynistic as it sung in praise of a woman who actually possesses some sort of personality and spunk. Of course the other interesting fact here is that Davy keeps singing about a woman weighs less than 100 lbs. Now Davy is notoriously short and may prefer a woman who is even shorter than himself, but whatever the height, 99 pounds seems a little on the anorexic side. Still Davy gets to do one of his big screaming "wow!" at the beginning of this song and keeps it churning throughout.

Jeff Barry hasn't yet come up with a suitable copy of "I'm A Believer" that will appease the single-buying Monkees audience. He's going to need Neil Diamond's help on that front, and so Neil pens the infectious **"A Little Bit Me, A Little Bit You"**. This is a bona-fide follow-up. The acoustic guitars are really brought to the front and the handclaps help propel the whole thing. The organ solo is great - in part because it is so quick. Davy's vocals may be a bit more cloying than Micky's would've been, but he does acquit himself quite nicely proving once again that he didn't have to just do slow ballads. Overall I find this song slightly less objectionable than "I'm A Believer" if only because it hasn't had any sort of *Shrek*-based revival. Although the song was a big hit single it never appeared on any official Monkees album as it was recorded after *More Of The Monkees*, yet would not have fit on *Headquarters* both ethically and musically.

The last song finished on this day by Jeff Barry was the infamous **"She Hangs Out"**. While this song would been re-done much more effectively for the *Pisces, Aquarius, Capricorn, & Jones, Ltd.* album, and here it sounds like any other song on this playlist. It is not as powerful or memorable as "A Little Bit Me, A Little Bit You", nor is it as bad as "You Can't Tie A Mustang Down." Really, it doesn't sound that much better or different than "99 Pounds." It's hard to decipher what exactly the lyrics are trying to say though. Is the narrator warning the girl that she might lose him to her sister unless she learns to dance like her sister? Or is the song trying to tell some woman that she should be concerned for her sister's safety? I'm not really sure either way. While Davy opens by asking how old her sister is, it's never made clear if this is a younger or elder sister that she needs to be concerned with. Mostly it comes across as creepy, as if the singer wants to make sure the sister is of a legal consenting age. At least it's not as bad as "Young Girl" by Gary Puckett & The Union Gap or Neil Diamond's own "Girl, You'll Be A Woman Soon."

Sure, Jeff Barry may have had his hand forced, but he did give Davy a few of the more rocking tunes to sing. Still something like **"Gotta Give It Time"** was going to require someone like Micky to really make it work. At the time however, Micky was boycotting Jeff Barry in solidarity with Mike and Peter. However time heals all wounds – or at least makes the reasons for such pettiness fuzzier. That's why in 2016, Micky finally added his vocals to this recording. Even Peter and Mike set aside their grudges and added some backing vocals, although given the sarcastic reading Nesmith gives his lines it may be that not all of his disdain for this music has dissipated. This is a pretty standard Jeff Barry production that is definitely on the more muscular side. Despite being a in his 70s, Micky sings it with a youthful gusto. It's nothing special, but it works pretty well.

While it was nice to hear Davy getting to sing the more rocking songs, of course Jeff Barry had to put him back into his safe, cuddly, romantic role for one last song. **"If I Learned To Play The Violin"** is pretty slow compared to the songs recorded five days previously, but most of the musicians remained and the song continues with the same organ-fronted band sound. The lack of the more obvious schmaltzy touches (including any actual violins) does help raise this song above the usual Davy ballad.

Lyrically the song is a little odd. It's all about the willingness to relinquish one's own personal values to please the girl in his life. Even worse, it's not so much the girl's as it is her parents' approval he is seeking. As part of the "young generation" who were making long-hair safe for television, it is a little sad to hear Davy treat this as just a meaningless rebellious phase that he needs to grow up and out of; that peace and love protesting the war and the whole counter-culture were just a clique that one could swap in and out of as the situation required. Of course, we have no idea if this is what the girl in question actually wants, or if she fell for the singer because he played the guitar instead of the violin. Not really the point, the singer just wanted to fit in with her friends and family.

It doesn't matter if this was recorded by Kirshner at the height of their feud or not, the sentiment of the lyric would've kept any of the other Monkees as far away from this as possible. This is probably the more safe-for-parents vein that Don Kirshner and the Powers-That-Be would've preferred the Monkees to continue in, but instead this would be the last thing that Jeff Barry did for the Monkees until nearly the very end of the whole phenomenon.

JEFF BARRY 3

1.) Oh My My 2:56
(written by Jeff Barry and Andy Kim)
from *Changes*
February 5th, 1970

2.) Tell Me Love 2:32
(written by Jeff Barry)
from *Changes*
February 5th, 1970

3.) I Love You Better 2:24
(written by Jeff Barry and Andy Kim)
from *Changes*
February 5th, 1970

4.) You're So Good To Me 2:27
(written by Jeff Barry and Bobby Bloom)
from *Changes*
March 25th, 1970

5.) Ticket On A Ferry Ride 3:20
(written by Jeff Barry and Bobby Bloom)
from *Changes*
March 25th, 1970

6.) All Alone In The Dark 2:46
(written by Ned Albright and Steven Soles)
from *Changes*
March 26th, 1970

7.) Do You Feel It Too? 2:27
(written by Jeff Barry and Andy Kim)
from *Changes*
March 26th, 1970

8.) It's Got To Be Love 2:19
(written by Neil Goldberg)
from *Changes*
April 2nd, 1970

9.) Acapulco Sun 2:47
(written by Ned Albright and Steven Soles)
from *Changes*
April 2nd, 1970

10.) Do It In The Name Of Love 2:08
(written by Neil Goldberg and Bobby Bloom)
released as a single
September 22nd, 1970

11.) Lady Jane 2:46
(written by Neil Goldberg and Bobby Bloom)
released as the b-side of the "Do It In The Name Of Love" single
September 22nd, 1970

Produced by Jeff Barry

MUSICIANS:
UNKNOWN

recorded 2/5/70 - 9/22/70

Once a former phenomenon has reached the depths that the Monkees' project had by 1970 there are only two options. One is to take advantage of the fact that no one is really paying attention to record your most weird and/or personal stuff. The other is to desperately do everything you can to crawl your way back to the top. This desperation usually takes one of two forms; either vainly hoping on the coattails of the latest trend or trying to replicate whatever it was that made them a success in the first place. What was left of the Monkees decided to go with the latter.

Without the objections of either Peter Tork or Michael Nesmith, it was pretty easy to welcome back into the fold former Kirshner henchman Jeff Barry. While Jeff did try to update their sound a bit to what has been described as "R&B meets bubblegum", mostly this was an attempt to duplicate past glories. The fact that several moldy outtakes from 1966/67 were included on the released album, *Changes*, belies this fact. So little effort or care was put into this album that no one seems to have taken note of which musicians actually played on these tracks.

Listening to the new material that Jeff Barry recorded at the time does give one an odd perspective on a potential alternate history in the Monkees universe. Suppose instead of firing Don Kirshner at that fateful crossroads back in early '67 the Powers-That-Be decided to hire someone like Dick Sergeant to wear the green wool cap and replace Nesmith on the TV show. The TV show probably would've continued on for several seasons until the fad naturally began to fade. Meanwhile competent, professional pop music like this would continue to be released under the Monkees' name. While the blow of Nesmith's departure might've hurt the band/show's popularity at the time, it probably would've been more financially beneficial for NBC and Colgems, at least in the short term. It is doubtful that the Monkees would've been remembered as fondly if they had continued in this vein, releasing albums such as *Changes*. Mostly likely no one would be taking the Monkees as seriously now and any reunions that might've happened in subsequent years would've only been enjoyed ironically, much like the *Brady Bunch* revival in the 1990's.

Legend has it that the tracks on this playlist were initially recorded for an Andy Kim album that never got released and then Jeff Barry's just replaced Andy's vocal tracks with Micky and Davy's. I didn't really know who Andy Kim is, so I was never really able to verify or comment on that possibility. So what I did is stream Andy's *Greatest Hits* compilation on Spotify. Dear God! This guy is like an even more milquetoast version of Neil Diamond. But I certainly can hear the similarities between his work and these tracks. Everything is very chipper. There is a lot of faux-funky electric piano and swinging, finger-snapping tempos with melodies that are designed to be as catchy as humanly possible but failing. Trust me; you don't want to listen to Andy Kim. It actually makes me appreciate Davy and Micky as vocalists that they could transform this material to anything that is listenable.

Despite the low opinion that most folks have of the album *Changes* it starts off really well with the single **"Oh My My"**. It opens with a great acoustic guitar riff played in an almost slap bass style. The general feel of the song is very slinky and cool. The lyrics are your typical "I've got a great woman and I will always love her" stuff. Despite the general disinterest that most of the participants showed in the making of this album, Micky sings it really well. While this is album is not as horrible as people imagine (in fact I think it's better than the first Jeff Barry playlist), it would've been a lot better if it had continued in this manner with just a little more enthusiasm applied.

"Tell Me Love" is a slow simmering ballad that is trying to be soulful like a gospel song. The backing vocals sound very Caucasian destroying any illusion that this song may be trying to create. The lyrics are pretty simple stuff, begging a girl to go out with the singer. Micky tries to add some smolder to his performance but it doesn't really work. It is not a bad song, but nothing really worth getting excited about.

"I Love You Better" is more funky bubblegum-soul. It's not nearly as effective as "Oh My My" but still not embarrassing. Micky is, as always, singing great. Even though Jeff Barry is back in charge, his preference for vocalists has switched from Davy to Micky. You can, however, hear Davy at least prominently in the backing vocals. Again this is nothing special, but all of the songs on this playlist do have the advantage of being pretty short and so they don't overstay their welcome. In fact, only one track on this whole playlist manages to get over three minutes.

Davy gets his first lead vocal with **"You're So Good To Me"**. Again the funk influence is evident, but this track also manages to get closer to the faux-gospel sound they were going for than "Tell Me Love". Davy does an okay job singing it, but it doesn't really seem like he's terribly invested in the lyrics, which are pretty banal if not actually annoying.

While there is a lot of R&B and soul going on here, **"Ticket On A Ferry Ride"** ends up sounding almost more like one of the more insipid ballads of CSN&Y, with its acoustic guitars and stacked vocal harmonies. This is the longest song here, and it does drag a bit. In fact the song could've very well ended at the break at three minutes in without really losing much without the repeated chorus for another twenty seconds. Again there's does seem to be a lot of effort put into these songs, so it's hard to put in the effort to come up with much to say about them.

"All Alone In The Dark" also sounds like there's someone singing along with Micky throughout the whole song. However here it isn't a harmony part, it's just the original vocals on the demo that songwriters submitted to Jeff Barry. Apparently Jeff Barry was either so enamored of this version or too lazy to bother, that he just had Micky overdub his vocals over the top of the demo without actually bother to re-record the song himself. Needless to say, it doesn't really sound like it fits in with the rest of the songs here. Still despite of this, "All Alone In The Dark" comes off pretty well. It's a goofy music hall kind of number with a fun little kazoo break and makes it a nice reprise from the other tracks on this playlist.

Davy's only other solo lead vocal here is **"Do You Feel It Too?"** This is far more typical of Davy. It's much more teen-oriented pop than any sort of blue-eyed soul. It chugs along amiably, and while the lyrics are standard fare, the only really annoying line involves life being groovy like a cartoon movie. Nothing on here has been a real dud yet, but this one certainly would not have been as forgivable if it were any longer than two and a half minutes.

"It's Got To Be Love" continues in the same direction as most of the previous songs. It is faux-soul with very white backing vocals and a decent Micky lead. While it was an okay formula to begin with, after this many songs it is starting to get old. While the final *Changes* album probably would've benefited from the more consistent overall sound without the interloper outtakes from previous albums, it doesn't add up to a terribly varied listen.

Luckily or unluckily, **"Acapulco Sun"** tries to do something different. It is a faux-Caribbean song that sounds about as authentic as The Beach Boys' "Kokomo." It almost comes off as semi-racist as that song. It's hard to tell if Jeff Barry meant this song to be a send-up of this genre, but Micky delivers it straight making seem like a failed attempt to truly capture these island rhythms. Even worse, there is a sound starting at about 2:45 that I have gotten used to editing out in my own head from having created so many mixtapes on low-quality cassettes as a kid. It is the sound of badly oxidized tape squeaking against the tape heads. And this is on the actual song as it was recorded and released. The fact they didn't just re-cut the song shows the amount of apathy that was rampant during the recording of these tracks.

The next two songs were actually recorded after the *Changes* album wrapped and were initially released as a single credited to Mickey [sic] Dolenz and Davy Jones. Yes, they did actually manage to misspell Micky's name on the record label. Clearly no one within the Powers-That-Be really cared what happened to the Monkees at this point. These songs might be considered outside of the scope of this book other than they have appeared as bonus tracks on all subsequent re-issues of the *Changes* album on CD. They certainly are of a piece with the other songs on this playlist being R&B crossed with bubblegum tracks produced by Jeff Barry.

The A-side, **"Do It In The Name Of Love"** is pretty unremarkable having already heard the other tracks here. After all these years it is nice to hear both of the Monkees most well-known vocalists actually sharing a duet for a change. It fits them both pretty well, although Micky seems to be holding back a bit to keep from blowing Davy's breathy vocals off the record completely. The solo section seems to be missing anyone or anything actually taking a solo other than a couple of "hey!"s from Micky. The song is stuck in a holding pattern at this point. If someone was really paying attention, something would've been overdubbed here.

"Lady Jane" is nominally better with Davy seeming more on equal footing with Micky here. The song has a cool slinky feel with some neat riffing from the lead acoustic guitar. Still, this song doesn't seem like a duet in any real sense of the word. This isn't two different singers arguing over the same girl alá "The Girl Is Mine." In fact the whole thing could've been all sung by just one person and would've made as much, if not more, sense. The lyrics aren't even particularly suited to either vocalist and seemed just divvied up randomly with Davy and Micky simply just swapping couplets. While the general apathy towards the Monkees at this point is a little sad to see, this isn't really a bad place to wrap up the entire Monkees original catalog.

CHIP DOUGLAS 1

1.) All Of Your Toys 3:09
(written by Bill Martin)
first released on *Missing Links Vol. 1*
January 16th, 1967

2.) The Girl I Knew Somewhere 2:35
(written by Michael Nesmith)
released as the b-side to the "A Little Bit Me, A Little Bit You" single
January 16th, 1967

3.) Sunny Girlfriend 2:31
(written by Michael Nesmith)
from *Headquarters*
February 23rd, 1967

4.) Band Six 0:40
(written by Davy Jones, Micky Dolenz, Peter Tork, and Michael Nesmith)
from *Headquarters*
March 2nd, 1967

5.) Randy Scouse Git 2:32
(written by Micky Dolenz)
from *Headquarters*
March 2nd, 1967

6.) You Told Me 2:23
(written by Michael Nesmith)
from *Headquarters*
March 3rd, 1967

7.) Zilch 1:06
(written by Davy Jones, Micky Dolenz, Peter Tork, and Michael Nesmith)
from *Headquarters*
March 3rd, 1967

8.) Forget That Girl 2:23
(written by Chip Douglas)
from *Headquarters*
March 7th, 1967

9.) Shades Of Gray 3:19
(written by Barry Mann and Cynthia Weil)
from *Headquarters*
March 16th, 1967

10.) Early Morning Blues and Greens 2:32
(written by Jack Keller and Diane Hildebrand)
from *Headquarters*
March 22nd, 1967

11.) For Pete's Sake 2:09
(written by Peter Tork and Joseph Richards)
from *Headquarters*
March 23rd, 1967

12.) No Time 2:07
(written by Davy Jones, Micky Dolenz, Peter Tork, and Michael Nesmith)
from *Headquarters*
March 28th, 1967

REMAKES RECORDED THESE SESSIONS:
I Can't Get Her Off My Mind (from "Boyce & Hart 1" released on *Headquarters*)
Mr. Webster (from "Boyce & Hart 2" released on *Headquarters*)
I'll Spend My Life With You (from "Boyce & Hart 2" released on *Headquarters*)

UNFINISHED SONGS FROM THESE SESSIONS:
Where Has It All Gone? (written by Michael Nesmith)
She's So Far Out She's In (written by Baker Knight)
Cripple Creek (traditional)
I Was Born In East Virginia (traditional)
Two-Part Invention In F Major (written by J.S. Bach)
Cantata & Fugue in C&W (written by Michael Nesmith)
Masking Tape (written by Barry Mann and Cynthia Weil)
… and various other instrumental jams and goofs

Produced by Chip Douglas

MUSICIANS:
MICHAEL NESMITH: pedal steel guitar, 12-string guitar, organ
DAVY JONES: tambourine, jawbone, maracas, etc.
MICKY DOLENZ: drums, guitar
PETER TORK: keyboards, 6-string guitar, bass, 5-string banjo

CHIP DOUGLAS: bass
JOHN LONDON: bass (on "The Girl I Knew Somewhere" & "All Of Your Toys")
VINCE DeROSA: french horn (on "Shades Of Gray")
FRED SEYKORA: cello (on "Shades Of Gray")
JERRY YESTER: additional guitar (on "No Time")
KEITH ALLISON: additional guitar (on "No Time")

Recorded 1/16/67 – 3/28/67

It was a pivotal moment in pop music history when Michael Nesmith smashed his fist through the wall and warned Don Kirshner's lawyer that "it could've been his face." While it has been debunked, the myth goes that Don Kirshner was giving them the song "Sugar Sugar" to record at the time. It does make for a great story because after being fired, Don Kirshner would go on to be right and have a hit with that song from the far more malleable and fictitious group, The Archies. While I am not generally a big fan of boy bands and pop starlets, I keep an eye on them hoping that one day, one them will have their comparable Nesmith-fist moment. Britney Spears shaving her head was as close as we have gotten since (and that was more personal meltdown than musical revolt). I don't know if Maurice Starr, Lou Pearlman, Simon Cowell and their ilk are just better at vetting their superstars beforehand to prevent any potential flare-ups - or have done a better job of silencing them after they start to raise objections, but I would really love to see Miley Cyrus or somebody just call a press conference and say "Fuck it! My real love is Scottish bagpipe music and that is all I'm going to be recording from now on."

Much like if Bob Denver insisted on having his own island, the Monkees were now going to make their own music. But first they needed a producer. At Michael's suggestion, they hired the bassist from the Turtles, a guy named Chip Douglas. Peter's suggestion was that they use Stephen Stills. Who knows how seriously the other three considered this, or if Stephen was even broached on the subject, but it did not happen. Possibly the Monkees, after having finally ousted Don Kirshner, didn't want any other strong personalities to butt heads with.

Chip on the other hand had never produced before. Perhaps the Monkees (particularly control-freak Nesmith) wanted someone a little unprepared to lead around. Plus Chip played bass, so they could free up Tork to play a myriad of other instruments while still keeping all of the playing in-house. It's hard to say percentage of the production is really Chip Douglas and how much is just an uneasy alliance between the Monkees themselves.

When the Monkees stopped playing on their own records and former producers were being lured back into the fold Chip tried to get himself rehired by recording tracks for the Monkees to potentially sing on, and paying for it out of his own pocket. Unfortunately, this failed to pay off for Chip. Only of these tunes, "Steam Engine", ever got finished, and then was left unreleased. This one song is the only glimpse we get into what a real Chip Douglas produced version of the Monkees would be like. Although the Chip Douglas produced backing tracks for something called "I'm A Man" as well a version of "We Were Made For Each Other" which is infinitely superior to the version produced by Davy. It has a somewhat folksy, country-ish feel and it is a shame that this version never received vocals. Hard to say what would've happened had Chip really been given a free hand to produce the Monkees the way say, Jeff Barry or Boyce & Hart did.

While "Steam Train" was a funky R&B number, the sound that the Monkees were trying to make was closer to folk-rock; namely, garage-band folk-rock. The Monkees had each been hired for their differing tastes and styles, so coming to a consensus amongst them was probably hard. Plus, they had not really been playing together as a band for very long. Micky had just learned the drums less than a year before. Needless to say this was going to be a rough, ragged recording. But *Headquarters* is a much more sincere and deeply felt Monkees album than anything that had been recorded or released by them up to this point.

This is another one of the playlists I created that most closely matches the released version of the album. The most notable differences are that I removed the re-recordings of the Boyce & Hart tunes that had appeared on previous playlists ("I'll Spend My Life With You", I Can't Get Her Off Of My Mind" and "Mr. Webster"). While I generally prefer the more stripped down sound of this record compared to Boyce & Hart's work, I don't think it's as effective on those three tracks as they were given the full Boyce & Hart treatment.

Another big, yet confusing, aspect to the sound of this record was Mike's decision to play pedal steel guitar on several tracks. Mike had been playing pedal steel for about as long as Micky played drums, so he wasn't very good yet. Luckily Michael knew his limitations on the instrument and tended to keep his parts very simple. However since there wasn't any pedal steel on previous Monkees releases, there was no need for him to play the instrument at all. Especially if they were trying to keep the sound consistent with the previous two releases. Since you saw Davy playing tambourine all the time on the TV show, he was now obligated to add percussion to almost every track on this record, despite not really caring at all about it. However you never saw Mike play pedal steel on the show or on stage or hardly even in photographs. So it's hard to figure out why he chose to complicate the recording process by insisting on playing it so much. He seems to have never played it again after this album was finished (perhaps because he struck up a friendship with O.J. "Red" Rhodes by this point and if he needed a pedal steel part he would just call his friend in to do it). Maybe Mike was just trying to keep the country influence that his songs provided on the first two records continuing through to this one.

The first song the Monkees tried by themselves was **"All Of Your Toys"**. This song was written by Bill Martin, who at the time was not signed to Screen Gems music publishing contract so there was no way that the Powers-That-Be were going to release the song and lose that potential revenue stream. It is often assumed that this was a mistake on the Monkees' part, but I don't that they were so oblivious. I think they felt safe trying to record this tune first, knowing there was no way it would see the light of day. They just wanted to experiment in the studio and see if what they were doing would work together: Peter's harpsichord, Mike's electric 12-string guitar, Micky's amateur drumming, Davy having to play some sort of percussion, the four of them doing all the backing vocals themselves. It also seems that they went out of their way to make sure all of this was used and highlighted with Peter's goofy count-in and Mike's backing vocals being turned up just to test out the formula and see what the potential obstacles would be.

As it is, the tune works out pretty well, but it is certainly a much different feel than anything that went out under the Monkees' name previously. If they thought they could sneak in a few tracks like this on the next album and it would blend in, they were sorely mistaken. This style here would never have worked as simply the b-sides to one of Jeff Barry's productions.

Still they were going really try for that b-side on their next song. Although written (and sung better) by Michael Nesmith, **"The Girl I Knew Somewhere"** features vocals by Micky as the group rightly figured Don Kirshner would not release a song on either side of a single if Mike (or Peter) sang it. While it has a very similar feel to "All Of Your Toys" being mostly harpsichord-driven, this track does work better by being a little less goofy and childish in the lyrics and the backing vocals being far less obtrusive. The 12-string guitar sounds almost like the Byrds here and Micky keeps his drum parts simple but effective. Davy's tambourine is turned down in the mix. A little of the Monkees sense of humor does sneak out in the off note deliberately thrown in at the end of Peter's harpsichord solo. Mike has reigned in his more idiosyncratic tendencies with the lyrics and has penned something fairly straight-forward and romance-based.

Mike was never terribly comfortably trying to write those kind of standard pop music lyrics. He always had a tendency to throw in verbose words like "propinquity" and odd line "this I'll avow ya." **"Sunny Girlfriend"** in some ways marks Mike's attempt to write in this genre with its subject limitations while still honoring his growing abilities as a wordsmith. While the song is ostensibly about a girlfriend (the word is right in the title) the rest of the lyrics are a lot more confused... or confusing. What is a "sunshine factory"? What do "eyes like thunder" look like? Mike was still trying at this point to straddle the line between satisfying Don Kirshner and his own muse. In the future Mike's lyrics would be divided into poems set to music like "Daily Nightly" and "Tapioca Tundra" and regular old love songs like "While I Cry" and "Good Clean Fun", but it is fascinating to hear him try and do both at the same time.

The song itself works wonderfully. This is one of the few tracks that Pete actually played bass on and his boogie-woogie line holds the whole thing together. The intro (cribbed from the Rolling Stones' "It's All Over Now") features some cool cymbal crashes from Micky that are either reversed or faded up. The whole thing is performed with a lot of energy and joy that probably comes from the Monkees enjoying the fact they've thrown off the shackles of Don Kirshner. While they did eventually grow tired of each other and the process of recording a whole album together, it doesn't really show in even the later performances from this playlist.

"Band Six" is not really a song. It's more of a statement from the Monkees that they were going to do their own thing in their own way on this album. Sure it's just a short botched attempt to play the Looney Tunes theme on the pedal steel guitar, but this is the kind of thing that wouldn't have even been saved on tape in the Kirshner days, much less put on the actual album. It is brief interludes like this and "Zilch" that really make the *Headquarters* album for me. When I am putting together my own playlist version of this album I will frequently add even more bits like "Six-String Improvisation" (later renamed "Cantata & Fugue in C&W" by Mike) or "Don't Be Cruel." The *Headquarters Sessions* box set gives us lots of these bits too choose from; perhaps too many. My favorite of all of them is a version of the traditional folk tune "I Was Born In East Virginia". With just Peter playing banjo. This is about the only time you get to hear Dolenz and Tork harmonizing like this. It sounds great and it's a shame that vocal blend wasn't employed more often.

"Randy Scouse Git" may or may not be the first song Micky has ever written; the pre-Monkees single "Don't Do It" is credited him although who knows how accurate that is. This is certainly one of the earliest songs he ever wrote. While Micky may have been most known as a child actor before his stint on the Monkees, he did play guitar and sing with a couple of local bands before getting the role of the Monkees drummer. While Micky may not have ever played drums before getting the gig, he learned well enough once he was cast. Still, he never had any real aspirations to be a rock-star much less an artist. Therefore Micky's songwriting attempts are interesting in an odd way, as an example of an inventive mind let loose in the studio with unlimited funds and imagination but a limited amount of experience in making his own music and very little preconceived notions of how to go about it. On the TV show, Micky is sometimes presented with a mad scientist demeanor that is an exaggerated version of how he was in real life.

On "Randy Scouse Git," Micky comes across a lot like the guy who built the gyrocopter in his basement; a little inelegant but brave in the way he put random parts together in order to construct what he thought of as a song. It is really cool in an almost outsider-art way, where you have to ignore a lot of technical naïveté in order to enjoy the inner genius. It's a good song, but not one that someone who has written a lot of songs would come up with. There are basically two parts to the song: the chirp-y, light verses, and the big tympani and shouting choruses. Then at the end he has both going on simultaneously... just to see what would happen. It's great. There's even a scat solo since there wasn't anything that Micky could play well enough for an instrumental break. It is trippy and far-out and there was no way Don Kirshner would've tolerated any of this. It is a bit of a relic of the times, but it still holds up great. The lyrics are free-form impressions that don't mean a lot unless Micky explains them to you, which he done often. Needless to say this would be the last song on the *Headquarters* album as released, because there is almost no way to follow-up after it.

Of the first five new songs recorded (not counting "Band Six") three were written by Michael Nesmith. Clearly he was the one who was most confident and had material ready to go. **"You Told Me"** is Mike going back to the romantic subject matter that was expected of the Monkees' songs. This is nowhere as cryptic as "Sunny Girlfriend", instead is another song about not being quite certain that the girl you're talking to is who she says she is or will end up breaking your heart. It is a common theme in Mike's more straightforward lyrics like "While I Cry" and "The Girl I Knew Somewhere." While Peter's harpsichord has been absent after the first two tracks recorded, he breaks out the banjo here to make his mark on the recording. It is another instrument that is not terribly typical in this kind of music that only Peter would try and push in this context. He certainly plays it so well that it actually works. The opening count-in is a bit of a goof on the beginning of the Beatles "Taxman" from *Revolver*. Other than that, it is pretty good but not terribly remarkably track. It is high energy but not nearly as cool as "Sunny Girlfriend."

"Zilch" is not really a song, but another behind-the-scenes glimpse like "Band Six." Sounding like a four-way tongue twister, it almost feels like a vocal exercise that the actors would do to prepare before shooting a scene of the TV show. It is rare to get equal vocals from all four Monkees, and it is fun to pick your favorite phrase and then try to keep up with the recording. While Kirshner may not have been amenable to this kind of tomfoolery on his albums, the Monkees would soon leave a spot for Peter to do something short and a Capella on future albums in an attempt to give him more of a vocal presence on the next few albums.

While to Don Kirshner and thousands of teenage girls at the time Davy was the lead singer for the Monkees, we're over halfway through this playlist before Chip Douglas and the rest recorded a lead vocal for Davy. **"Forget That Girl"** is a pretty straightforward, drippy ballad bolstered by the stripped-down production, particularly Peter Tork's electric piano. It's hard to say if Davy's marginalization on this album was due to the fact they saw him as something of a turncoat for collaborating with Jeff Barry. Maybe he just hadn't bonded as much as the other three during the making of this album as his tambourine and maraca playing was not terribly essential to the recording and he was not interested in the process of being an artiste like the other three. Most likely they were just not sure what material to record for him as he was not writing his own tunes and they would need to turn to Don Kirshner's stable of Brill Building writers to find material suitable for him. Whatever the reason this is fairly standard Davy song that works okay but is not worth getting excited about.

Luckily, **"Shades Of Grey"** is much better. Davy actually shares the lead vocals here with a Peter Tork. While Davy's voice is prettier, Peter gives this song a plaintiveness that would've been missing if Davy sang it by himself. However, Davy's presence does add a smooth and more universal entrance to this song and it works better because both of them are singing it. The arrangement is simple but effective. Micky's drumming, with mostly just snare punctuations, is a great use of his limited abilities. Mike's very rudimentary pedal steel playing does not seem country-ish at all, but adds to the overall stately sound. The horn and cello parts were played by professionals but written by Mike and notated by Peter. The lyrics are a sad reflection on the complexities of growing older without being too maudlin or whiny. This is simply a lovely song.

"Early Morning Blues & Greens" is the third song in a row with Davy on lead vocals. In recent years Peter has stated that he would've loved to have sung this song instead and that he should've fought harder for the chance. It would've been an interesting choice, and probably a better one, but that would leave Davy - the ostensible star of the show - with very little to sing on this album, mostly remakes of previously unreleased songs. As it is, "Early Morning Blues & Greens" is a better version of "Forget That Girl". Once again Peter's keyboard playing is prominent, and the spooky horror-house organ solo he does is great, if a little out of character for the rest of the song. The lyrics are an odd change of pace for Davy; instead of being about falling love it seems to be about struggling to get out of bed in the morning. There is also this weird clashing sound that sounds somewhere between a cymbal and someone hitting a trash-can lid that punctuates the whole song. Much like the organ solo it does seem out of place, but makes the track sound much more interesting than it would've been had it just been another typical Davy ballad.

While Mike and Micky's songs were some of the first recorded, Peter's first real songwriting credit, **"For Pete's Sake"** gets pushed to nearly the end. Furthermore Peter's over-generosity ends up giving his roommate co-writing credit for coming up with just a few lines. Pete doesn't even get to sing his own song, although Micky does a stellar job singing it. You would think that freed from Kirshner's control, Peter would've been able to make bigger strides towards getting a chance to sing lead on this album.

Peter should've at least been able to write more material for *Headquarters*. Clearly it was a matter of confidence and not talent as the song here is phenomenal and was understandably chosen as the closing theme for the second season of the TV show. The main guitar riff features some ninth chords that are much more sophisticated than the types of chords Mike usually used. The lyrics are pretty typical "love & peace" stuff, but isn't as dated or embarrassing as most of the more "hippie" material that was being recorded around this time. The rather simple stabs of the organ here are provided by Mike who also came up with the title for this track. It is a great song that is a lot more complicated or sophisticated than one would have expected from a young, inexperienced folk-rock garage band.

"No Time" on the other hand is exactly the kind of thing you would expect from a band still learning how to play together. Not that this is an insult, but it is a very simple song that sounds more bashed together than like anyone wrote it. Which is apparently is what happened. It's just a Chuck Berry style jam that Micky and Mike came up with some ridiculous lyrics for. The Monkees credited the song to Hank Cialo in thanks for engineering the album. Surprisingly, Peter chokes halfway through the piano solo and Micky throws in a drum fill to save the day. However, Davy's backing vocals on this song may be the best thing he did for the entire *Headquarters* album. He sounds like he's about to go completely mad mixed down there screaming "no time no time at all." This song sounds like a lot of fun to play, and that really shows through on the performance. This is good because the song itself is so flimsy as to be barely anything at all. This is the kind of tune that if it had been recorded by disinterested profession sidemen would've come off as desperately pretending to be having a good time. However the freedom to do something so simple and stupid on a real major album is infectious and listening to the Monkees bash their way through it is great.

CHIP DOUGLAS 2

1.) Cuddly Toy 2:39
(written by Harry Nilsson)
from *Pisces, Aquarius, Capricorn, & Jones, Ltd.*
April 26th, 1967

2.) Peter Percival Patterson's Pet Pig Porky 0:27
(written by Peter Tork)
from *Pisces, Aquarius, Capricorn, & Jones, Ltd.*
June 10th, 1967

3.) Pleasant Valley Sunday 3:16
(written by Gerry Goffin and Carole King)
from *Pisces, Aquarius, Capricorn, & Jones, Ltd.*
June 10th, 1967

4.) Salesman 2:37
(written by Craig Vincent Smith)
from *Pisces, Aquarius, Capricorn, & Jones, Ltd.*
June 14th, 1967

5.) Daydream Believer 3:01
(written by John Stewart)
from *Pisces, Aquarius, Capricorn, & Jones, Ltd.*
June 14th, 1967

6.) Love Is Only Sleeping 2:32
(written by Barry Mann and Cynthia Weil)
from *Pisces, Aquarius, Capricorn, & Jones, Ltd.*
June 19th, 1967

7.) Daily Nightly 2:33
(written by Michael Nesmith)
from *Pisces, Aquarius, Capricorn, & Jones, Ltd.*
June 19th, 1967

8.) What Am I Doing Hanging Around? 3:09
(written by Michael Martin Murphey and Owen Castleman)
from *Pisces, Aquarius, Capricorn, & Jones, Ltd.*
June 20th, 1967

9.) Don't Call On Me 2:53
(written by Michael Nesmith and John London)
from *Pisces, Aquarius, Capricorn, & Jones, Ltd.*
June 20th, 1967

10.) Goin' Down 4:26
(written by Diane Hildebrand, Davy Jones, Micky Dolenz, Peter Tork, and Michael Nesmith)
released as a b-side to the "Daydream Believer" single
June 21st, 1967

11.) Star Collector 4:32
(written by Gerry Goffin and Carole King)
from *Pisces, Aquarius, Capricorn, & Jones, Ltd.*
June 22nd, 1967

12.) The Door Into Summer 2:51
(written by Bill Martin and Chip Douglas)
from *Pisces, Aquarius, Capricorn, & Jones, Ltd.*
August 23rd, 1967

13.) Hard To Believe 2:37
(written by Davy Jones, Kim Capli, Eddie Brick, and Charlie Rockett)
from *Pisces, Aquarius, Capricorn, & Jones, Ltd.*
August 23rd, 1967

14.) Riu Chiu 1:33
(Traditional)
first released on *Missing Links Vol. II*
August 24th, 1967

15.) Special Announcement 0:39
(written by Davy Jones, Micky Dolenz, Peter Tork, and Michael Nesmith)
first released as a bonus track on *Pisces, Aquarius, Capricorn, & Jones, Ltd.*
October 9th, 1967

REMAKES RECORDED THESE SESSIONS:
Words (from "Boyce & Hart 2" released on *Pisces, Aquarius, Capricorn, & Jones, Ltd.*)
She Hangs Out (from "Jeff Barry 2" released on *Pisces, Aquarius, Capricorn, & Jones, Ltd.*)

UNFINISHED SONGS FROM THESE SESSIONS:
The Story Of Rock And Roll (written by Harry Nilsson)
Yours Until Tomorrow (written by Gerry Goffin and Carole King)

Produced by Chip Douglas

MUSICIANS:

MICHAEL NESMITH: guitar

PETER TORK: keyboards, organ, piano

EDDIE HOH: drums, percussion

CHIP DOUGLAS: guitar, bass, backing vocals

MICKY DOLENZ: drums (on "Cuddly Toy"), moog synthesizer (on "Daily Nightly")

PAUL BEAVER: moog synthesizer (on "Star Collector")

DAVY JONES: percussion

DOUG DILLARD: electric banjo (on "What Am I Doing Hangin' 'Round?")

BILL CHADWICK: acoustic guitar (on "Pleasant Valley Sunday")

BILL MARTIN: percussion (on "Daydream Believer")

NATHAN KAPROFF, GEORGE KAST, ALEX MURRAY & ERNO NEUFELD: violin (on "Daydream Believer")

PETE CANDOLI, AL PORCINO & MANUEL STEVENS: trumpet (on "Daydream Believer")

RICHARD NOEL: trombone (on "Daydream Believer")

RICHARD LEITH & PHILIP TEELE: bass trombone (on "Daydream Believer")

PETE CANDOLI, AL PORCINO & MANNY STEVENS: trumpet (on "She Hangs Out")

DICK NOEL: trombone (on "She Hangs Out")

DICK LEITH & PHIL TEELE: bass trombone (on "She Hangs Out")

SHORTY ROGERS: arrangement (on "Daydream Believer" and "Goin' Down")

TED NASH, THOMAS SCOTT & BUD SHANK: reeds, winds (on "Cuddly Toy")

EDGAR LUSTGARTEN: cello (on "Cuddly Toy")

KIM CAPLI: guitar, piano, bass, drums, shaker, cowbell, claves & other percussion (on "Hard To Believe")

VINCENT DeROSA: french horn (on "Hard To Believe")

OLLIE MITCHELL & TONY TERRAN: flugelhorn (on "Hard To Believe")

BOBBY KNIGHT: bass trombone (on "Hard To Believe")

JIM HORN: baritone sax (on "Hard To Believe")

LEONARD ATKINS, ARNOLD BELNICK, NATHAN KAPROFF, WILBERT NUTTYCOMBE, JEROME REISLER & DARRELL TERWILLIGER: violin (on "Hard To Believe")

BUD BRISBOIS, VIRGIL EVANS, UAN RASEY & THOMAS SCOTT: trumpet (on "Goin' Down")

BOBBY HELFER: trumpet, bass clarinet (on "Goin' Down")

LOU BLACKBURN & DICK NASH: trombone (on "Goin' Down")

DICK LEITH & PHIL TEELE: bass trombone (on "Goin' Down")

BUDDY COLLETTE, BILL HOOD & PLAS JOHNSON: sax (on "Goin' Down")

JOHN LOWE: bass sax, bass clarinet (on "Goin' Down")

Recorded 4/26/67 – 10/16/67

It may say something about Micky's drumming that simply switching from him to session musician Eddie Hoh makes *Pisces, Aquarius, Capricorn, & Jones, Ltd.* sound so much more polished and professional. It almost sounds like they switched back to using nothing but session musicians for everything for this album. This can be both a good and a bad thing. Certainly Peter, Mike, and Chip have been playing together longer by now and have gelled quite a bit more. In addition, not having the frustrations of waiting for Micky or Davy to do a good take may have allowed them more freedom to get their own parts right. It is also worth noting is that Mike had put his pedal steel guitar away for this album adding to the less amateurish sound overall.

While *Pisces, Aquarius, Capricorn, & Jones, Ltd.* both as released and the playlist here sound much better than their predecessor, a lot of the charm and the character has been lost. This no longer has that all-for-one, we'll-show-'em spirit. Instead it is also a much bigger opportunity for Mike to make the kind of Monkees album that he always wanted to make. Mike sings lead on five of the songs, all of which were released on the original album. Meanwhile Peter is still relegated to the sidelines vocally, only getting to do funny short spoken words bits that match his on-screen character as well as half a lead vocal with a remake of "Words" from the Boyce & Hart days.

This playlist is even closer to the actual released album than the last one. The main difference is the exclusion of the two remakes on this album; the aforementioned "Words" and a re-do of Jeff Barry's "She Hangs Out". I noticed that on the last album the only tunes they deemed worthy of re-recording were Boyce & Hart tunes. By the time of *PiscesI*, relations between the cast and Don Kirshner must've thawed a bit as they were willing to do a song by his right-hand man Jeff Barry. Unlike the previous remakes, the Jeff Barry tune actually benefits from the improvements that the Monkees' arrangement adds to it. That version is significantly better than the one that Don Kirshner got fired for releasing as a b-side in Canada. As for the Boyce & Hart number, the arrangements are so close to the original it is hard to detect which one is the professional studio musicians and which one is the actual Monkees. The main change in the arrangement is swapping out the flute solo for an organ solo and removing the dated sounding bit of tape rewinding. Both decisions were improvements, although overall they come across as about the same.

The first song here, **"Cuddly Toy"** may in fact belong more with the previous playlist than it does on this one. It was recorded less than a month after "No Time" but almost two months before "Pleasant Valley Sunday". Micky is still drumming on this track and I certainly have waffled back and forth over with chapter to include this song in. I finally decided to put it here as it was intended for and officially released on *Pisces, Aquarius, Capricorn, & Jones, Ltd.* This is another music hall type song for Davy, but if you're going to do this kind of thing, you can't really beat the master of this genre: Harry Nilsson. The lyrics are supposedly inspired by a Hell's Angels gang-rape, but you would never know by listening to them. This is the perfect soft-shoe type number for Davy, standing heads and shoulders above the Herman's Hermits-style stuff that Boyce & Hart would have him sing.

"Peter Percival Patterson's Pet Pig Porky" is not rally song but a short spoken word piece that shows off Peter's ability to pop the letter "p" whilst reciting a silly tongue twister. This "song" is credited to Pete as the songwriter, but even he will admit wasn't actually written by him as much as it was just taught to him. While on *Headquarters* tracks such as this were included to give the listener an intimate sense of the record being made. On *Pisces*, this track seems included just to remind that Peter was still a part of the Monkees. Much like "Your Auntie Grizelda", this is clearly more tailored to Peter Tork, the TV character, than it is for Peter Tork, the actual human being. Since this is just a solo a Capella bit and as such isn't the camaraderie of such tracks as "Zilch" or "Band Six." Still it is nice that they threw Peter a bone and put this on the actual record.

Opening with a guitar riff admittedly cribbed from the Beatles' "I Want To Tell You", **"Pleasant Valley Sunday"** is as solidly constructed perfect pop single as "Last Train To Clarksville" or "I'm A Believer." As great as this record undeniably is, there's not much to say about it. The most impressive thing about it is that this it proves that the Monkees as musicians could pull it off themselves. By this point they didn't need the studio musicians and this track does not stick out when placed amongst the other songs on a Greatest Hits compilation.

"Pleasant Valley Sunday" is surprisingly equanimous as it gives each of the Monkees individually to shine. Dolenz sings his heart out, but Mike hold his own with the harmony. But when it comes for the wordless "ta-da-da" bridge, only Davy could have done it as convincingly. While Peter is not heard singing, his piano playing really holds the song together, especially on the bridge. While I tend to prefer songs that have a bit more weirdness to them, of all the straight-forward smash hit tunes that the Monkees have, this might be my favorite.

Pisces, Aquarius, Capricorn, & Jones, Ltd. features the most lead vocals by Michael of any released Monkees' album, yet he only wrote two of the songs on it; one of which Micky sings and the other is co-written. Mike was clearly relishing the chance to sing other people's songs on this album. **"Salesman"** is the first of these songs that he didn't write it himself. Somehow it still sounds like a quintessential Nesmith track. "Salesman" was actually written by Craig Vincent Smith of the band Penny Arkade whose record, *Not The Freeze*, Michael was producing at this time. Though that album was never really finished, it is a great listen for the country-and-psychedelia mash-up that Mike was working in at the time. When Craig did release his version of the song as Maitreya Kali on the *Apache Inca* album you can hardly hear the song over the taped dialogue of Beach Boy Mike Love just talking, which is really too bad because what you can hear is pretty cool.

As recorded by Chip Douglas and the Monkees, "Salesman" prominently features an instrument that got a lot of use during these sessions: the nylon string guitar. The lyrics are somewhat disdainful yet still sympathetic to its haggard huckster. Musically it is just a variation on your standard I-IV-V 12-bar blues with a sort of Tex-Mex feel. The backing vocals are a great taunting counterpoint. The whole song is rollicking, and the only thing that keeps this track from standing out is that there are number of other tunes just as good on this playlist.

"Daydream Believer" starts with a short exchange between Davy and producer Chip Douglas that brings to mind the more informal sound of *Headquarters*. However this song sounds far more professional or polished than anything off of that album. While the horns and strings threaten to turn this song into schmaltz, the solid sympathetic backing by Chip, Mike, Peter, and Eddie Hoh actually keep this song from being too saccharine. "Daydream Believer" is not nearly as good as "Pleasant Valley Sunday", but holds up pretty well alongside the other big sellers in the Monkees' catalogue. It certainly is the better of the two huge songs that Monkees recorded with the word "believer" in the title.

The most notable thing about this song is although recorded during *Pisces, Aquarius, Capricorn, & Jones, Ltd.* it was deliberately held back for the next album, *The Birds, The Bees, & The Monkees* just to ensure that the subsequent album also had a smash hit on it. This was pretty prescient of the Powers-That-Be as the commercial prospects for the Monkees were about become quite confused after this album, after Chip Douglas is ousted and each of the four Monkees wandering off to do their own thing.

While both "Daydream Believer" and "Pleasant Valley Sunday" were obvious choices for the single, for a short while **"Love Is Only Sleeping"** was actually considered for the a-side. Eventually this song was deemed too risqué. Certainly the other two songs proved themselves as commercially. Still it would've been a brave and strong choice if the Powers-That-Be had put it out. First off, it would've been the first a-side not to feature either Davy or Micky on the vocals. Secondly the song is rather odd and angular with large chunks of it in an off-putting 7/8 time. Despite the tricky rhythm, Micky actually originally played drums on this track before having his part added to by "Fast" Eddie Hoh. I'm not sure how much of what's on the record Micky played, but that is still pretty impressive.

This is one of my favorite Monkees' songs, with the guitar riff pulling together the otherwise wonky feel. Mike's voice is extraordinarily expressive on this song, sometimes whispering, sometimes pleading, handling a large range with an amazing ease. The song ends with reverb being added increasingly to the track until everything is drowned out. This is a trick that was also used on "Pleasant Valley Sunday" and a couple of others on this playlist. It is a clever way of ending a song that doesn't have an ending written without resorting to just fading the track out.

On the only song Mike wrote by himself for this album, **"Daily Nightly"**, he has given up on writing lyrics about love or that even make sense. There are some pretty cool turns of phrase in here, but if someone didn't tell you that it was related to the riots at a nightclub in L.A. at the time, you couldn't decipher it on your own. This is one of the few songs that Mike wrote that there has been no unearthed versions of Mike actually singing it himself, "Mary Mary" being the other. It would be interesting to hear his vocal take on this song, but as it is Micky handles the tricky phonetics and elastic melody with aplomb. The vocals are not, however, Micky's most notable contribution to this song.

Sometime in 1967 Micky had acquired one of the first ever synthesizers from Moog and despite not really knowing how to play it, or even how it worked, he went ahead and added a surreal series of swoops and screeches to the tune. There are times when I will admit that I found these sounds distracting and would prefer to hear the "real" song underneath by itself. That said, it takes what would've been a fairly unremarkable and probably forgotten album cut and transports it into outer space. While this sonic experimentation makes "Daily Nightly" very progressive, I think it's too bad that this track is remembered more for that element rather than the actual song itself.

From the extremely futuristic "Daily Nightly" Mike goes for the extremely traditional country tune **"What Am I Doing Hangin' 'Round?"** Despite the fact that Peter is an extremely talented banjo picker, Chip and Mike went with the world famous Douglas Dillard to play on this track, perhaps as a deliberate snub to Tork. The tune is for the most part very straight-forward except for the leap up to the E flat. This is a very typical Michael Nesmith chord trick, but the song is in fact written by Michael Martin Murphey of "Wildfire" fame. The lyrics, which are a wistful regret of loving and then leaving a young girl in Mexico, could easily have come off as mean-spirited (just imagine Davy singing it), but it doesn't rankle as much in Mike's hands. While Mike kept his country leanings satisfied by busying himself with the pedal steel on the last record, here it jumps to the forefront. Undiluted, this country song feels a bit out-of-place amongst its peers on this playlist.

While "What Am I Doing Hangin' Round?" is pure country, **"Don't Call On Me"** is pure lounge. While the term lounge music is often used pejoratively when describing music, bringing to mind images of Bill Murray singing the Star Wars theme on *SNL*, it doesn't necessarily have to be this way. As much as Michael was brought up on Hank Williams and Bo Didley, another big influence on him when he was young was Xavier Cugat. You can hear a lot of that in here. Mike, who rarely uses complex jazz chords, opens up with a pair of major sevenths. The whole thing is delivered unironically. However, the Monkees must've realized how "square" this track must've seemed and added some opening and closing chatter to the recording to sort of wink at this audience to let them know that they too are in on the joke. It sorts of feels like the canned laughter at the end of the Beatles' "Within You Without You."

The song is co-credited to Mike and his long time bassist John London on *Pisces, Aquarius, Capricorn, & Jones, Ltd.* On the 1968 big band experiment, *The Wichita Train Whistle Sings*, Mike is listed as the sole author. Maybe Mike just gave John co-writing credit on the Monkees album in gratitude to John, or maybe Mike ripped John off on *Wichita Train Whistle*. On that version, the end of the phrase is never played and maybe that's the part that John London added. Who knows? As odd as the song is, it was actually written pre-Monkees. There is a demo version out there from that time, which while more lo-fi and missing that spoken intro/outro does sound very similar to the released version. On another interesting note, you can hear Peter and Mike jam briefly on this tune acoustically on the episode "Monkee Mother" in the scene where the set Rose Marie up on a date.

"Going Down" is to *Pisces, Aquarius, Capricorn, & Jones, Ltd.* what "No Time" was to *Headquarters*. Another simple four chord jam with some lyrics added on later. While "No Time" was raucous, "Going Down" is a little smoother, thanks in part to Eddie's drumming as well as the addition of a horn section which was over-dubbed later. What truly makes this song special is the speed at which Micky spits out all these lyrics. It is truly impressive, and is kind of fun to see how long one can sing along before running out of breath. Micky however never seems to be straining as he rattles off this somewhat macabre tale of trying to drown himself over a lost love and instead finding that he is floating and learning to accept his fate. It is a great fun song, so it's kind of a surprise that it wasn't actually released on *Pisces*, but was relegated to the b-side of the "Daydream Believer" single.

Next is **"Star Collector"** a three-chord shuffle with dismissive lyrics about a gold-digging groupie. Unlike "(I'm Not Your) Stepping Stone" the protagonist here seems far more interested in putting her down than standing up for himself. Davy's nasal vocals make the words even more dismissive and nasty. The song ends with the same type of "we don't have an ending jam" as "Lovely Rita" from *Sgt. Pepper*. This may have necessitated putting "Star Collector" at the end of *Pisces* as it would be hard for anything to come after it. The most notable part of this recording is that it's another example of some early synthesizer work. This time played it is played by Paul Beaver, someone who actually knows how to operate the Moog synthesizer. As such, Paul contributes something far more musical, but far less interesting, to the proceedings than Micky brought to "Daily Nightly."

Another lovely song sung by not written by Mike, **"The Door Into Summer"** suffers a little bit from being overshadowed by the other songs on this playlist. Once again the nylon string guitar rears its head. Micky does a lovely job with the harmony/backing vocals. The lyrics, while not as deep as they'd like to be, are not distracting or embarrassing. The main riff is a nice little confection, if not terribly infectious. It's really a shame that such a good song is surrounded by such great songs that it tends to feel a little redundant in the shuffle.

While "Don't Call On Me" is an example of good lounge music, **"Hard To Believe"** is an example of everything that is stereotypically wrong with this genre. It is cheezy elevator muzak. Davy, who was seeing how much money there was in writing Monkees music, obviously wanted to jump on the bandwagon. But it is doesn't seem to be out of any artistic expression but to line his pocketbook. While the rest of the songs on this playlist have pretty much the same group of musicians on them, this track pretty much is just co-writer Kim Capli playing everything except for the horns and strings that are drenched over the top. There are a couple of tunes that stick out on this playlist, but this one is the most egregious outsider. Not that it is horrible, but it feels out-of-whack and sadly mercenary. The only real bright spot in the tune is the very last note Davy sings when he unexpectedly breaks into harmony with himself on the word "you." This song makes "Don't Call On Me" and its ability to be lounge without being terrible seem that much more impressive.

While no Monkees played on "Hard To Believe," none of them played on **"Riu Chiu"** either. However this song was recorded a Cappella so it makes sense. Whatever people may say about the Monkees abilities as instrumentalists, their prowess as vocalists is really on full display here. Even Peter's voice sounds fantastic. The song is ostensibly a Xmas tune, although not one that has been done to death. Since most of the Monkees fan-base don't speak the language the lyrics are in, it is easy to appreciate even outside of the holiday season. While the song was recorded specifically for the TV show and not meant for release on record it is one of the most powerful songs they ever committed to tape.

Sessions for *Pisces, Aquarius, Capricorn, & Jones, Ltd.* ended pretty much the way they started (with the exception of "Cuddly Toy"). **"Special Announcement"** is another short comical spoken word segment by Peter Tork. Unlike "Peter Percival Patterson's Pet Pig Porky", this was not included on the record as released. Perhaps it was a little too "inside" with most listeners who are not being familiar with the tape alignment and VU meters that are being satirized. Or maybe that thought just one of these types of numbers were enough for the album. It is just a one-joke bit, and the joke isn't very funny, although however is doing the dog sounds does a great job. Still it would've been nice to have a little more vocal participation from Peter before Chip Douglas left and all the Monkees were forced to fend for themselves.

MICHAEL NESMITH 1

1.)   All The King's Horses 2:18
(written by Michael Nesmith)
first released on *Missing Links Vol. II*
June 25th, 1966

2.)   The Kind Of Girl I Could Love 1:50
(written by Michael Nesmith and Roger Atkins)
from *More Of The Monkees*
June 25th, 1966

3.)   I Don't Think You Know Me 2:17
(written by Gerry Goffin and Carole King)
first released on *Missing Links Vol. I*
June 25th, 1966

4.)   Papa Gene's Blues 1:58
(written by Michael Nesmith)
from the Monkees' debut album
July 7th, 1966

5.)   So Goes Love 3:08
(written by Gerry Goffin and Carole King)
first released on *Missing Links Vol. I*
July 7th, 1966

6.)   You Just May Be The One 2:00
(written by Michael Nesmith)
first released on *Missing Links Vol. II*
July 18th, 1966

7.)   Sweet Young Thing 1:55
(written by Gerry Goffin, Carole King, and Michael Nesmith)
from the Monkees' debut album
July 18th, 1966

8.) I Won't Be The Same Without Her 2:42
(written by Gerry Goffin and Carole King)
first released on *Instant Replay*
July 18th, 1966

9.) (I Prithee) Do Not Ask For Love 2:57
(written by Michael Martin Murphey)
first released on *Missing Links Vol. II*
July 25th, 1966

10.) Of You 1:58
(written by Bill Chadwick)
first released on *Missing Links Vol. I*
July 25th, 1966

11.) Mary, Mary 2:15
(written by Michael Nesmith)
from *More Of The Monkees*
July 25th, 1966

UNFINISHED SONGS FROM THESE SESSIONS:
Gonna Buy Me A Dog (written by Tommy Boyce and Bobby Hart)

Produced by Michael Nesmith

MUSICIANS:
JAMES BURTON, GLEN CAMPBELL, AL CASEY, MIKE DEASY &
    PETER TORK: guitar
BOB WEST: bass
HAL BLAINE: drums
LARRY KNECHTEL: keyboards, piano
GARY COLEMAN & JIM GORDON: percussion
DONALD PEAKE: conductor
MICHAEL COHEN: keyboards (on "Mary, Mary", "Of You", and "(I Prithee) Do Not Ask For
    Love")
JIM HELMS: guitar (on "Papa Gene's Blues")
BILL PITMAN: bass (on "So Goes Love" and "Papa Gene's Blues")
JIMMY BRYANT: fiddle (on "Sweet Young Thing")
FRANK DeVITO: percussion (on "Sweet Young Thing", "I Won't Be The Same Without Her", and
    "You Just May Be The One")
BILLY PRESTON: electric piano (on "So Goes Love")
LARRY KNETCHEL, MICHAEL NESMITH, MICKY DOLENZ, DAVY JONES & PETER
    TORK: backing vocals

Recorded 6/25/66 - 7/25/66

It seems that Michael was either led to believe or over-estimated the role he would have in recording of the Monkees albums. Don Kirshner's plan was that he was going to be treated like George Harrison, where he got to write and sing two tracks per released album but never on a single. However, no one told Mike about this and he seems to have thought that he was going to be producing most, if not all, of the album himself. He didn't just produce songs for himself to write and sing - but recorded a couple of songs written by some of Michael's friends as well as a few taken from Don Kirschner's stable of songwriters (mostly Goffin & King). He even produced a tune written by Boyce & Hart ("Gonna Buy Me A Dog" which never got around to getting vocals recorded on it). Michael probably wouldn't have been spending time on "So Goes Love" for Davy to sing if he didn't think he was going to be doing more than just a track or two. Once the first album came out and Michael saw what a diminished role he was really going to have on the records he didn't even bother to record more tunes for the second album since he knew he already had enough tracks in the can for Don Kirshner to choose from.

And the album that Michael thought he was producing for the Monkees would've been a much better album, if not as commercial as what Boyce & Hart were doing. On the officially released albums Mike's songs always felt like uncomfortable outsiders with little to nothing in common with the rest of the songs surrounding them. While the country influence is one of the first things remarked upon by listeners, there is also a distinct Latin influence that is noticeable. Perhaps Michael just wanted to make sure there were plenty of maracas for Davy to mime along to on the TV show, but there was always plenty of percussion on all of these tracks.

While there definitely a consistent twang-y, Latin feel to all these tracks, they do reach across a broad spectrum. The sound here is comprised mostly from a band that was eventually dubbed "The Wrecking Crew." This was the notorious group of session musicians regularly employed by Phil Spector and the Beach Boys to play on their recordings, and is often the group of session musicians that is credited with playing all of the Monkees music -- although clearly this was not the case. This bit of misinformation has not to be rectified by the surviving members of The Wrecking Crew, and occasionally has even been reinforced by them now that they no longer are content being paid union scale and then uncredited, but instead recognized as having played on many of the greatest hits of this era.

Michael did throw in Peter Tork on "fourth chair guitar" into this group, mostly as a consolation prize to Peter. Much like Boyce & Hart, Mike was never sure what to do with Peter's voice, although if Boyce & Hart hadn't finished their version of "Gonna Buy Me A Dog" first, Mike might have had Peter singing lead on the backing track he recorded for this tune. It certainly would've fit in with the comic persona Peter played on the TV show and his sometimes weak vocals would not have diminished what would've been nothing more than a novelty track. As far as I know Mike has not said anything about it one way or the other, although Mike was pretty big on having the three other guys and himself providing the backing vocals for all of these tunes as well as the leads.

The lead vocals on **"All The King's Horses"** are provided by Micky, but Mike provides a second vocal throughout which creates a very nice blend where it is somewhat difficult to determine who is really singing lead. In fact, only the last line is sung alone by Micky - but still it is important to note that his Mike doesn't technically sing lead on his first production for the Monkees. The song is very emblematic of the tone of this playlist. While the lyrics are pretty standard boy-girl fare, the "Humpty Dumpty" imagery is a nice twist. The drums are driving while the percussion is vaguely Latin and the guitar fills have a certain country twang to them. While this song might not have been used by Don Kirshner for the album, it was employed by Bob & Bert for the TV show. It certainly is a lot more sophisticated than the usual pop formula of the time.

However, in order to appease Don Kirshner's pop formula Mike was asked to try and learn the art of conventional songwriting by co-writing a few tracks with some proven professionals. **"The Kind Of Girl I Could Love"** was co-written by Roger Atkins, who was touted by Kirshner on the liner notes of *More Of The Monkees* as the lyricist for "It's My Life". He also co-wrote a couple of songs with Neil Sedaka, but is larger forgotten no outside of Brill Building aficionados. This forced songwriting arrangement couldn't have been very comfortable for Mike; but the song the came up with together sounds veryy Nesmith-y. The guitar sounds like it was recorded a little too hot and distorts a bit at the beginning, but the toms on here are great and the whole thing rocks along like a country-tinged Buddy Holly tune. The slide guitar is a great touch and the backing vocals (especially on the alternate mix) are wonderful.

Both Mike and Micky take a shot at singing lead on **"I Don't Think You Know Me At All"**, and while Mike may have done the better job of it, I usually listen to Micky's version as it gives more vocal equanimity to this playlist. Either way, this recording of the song is very different from the way that the songwriters Goffin & King produced it. Mike's version remains in the vaguely experimental mode of adding a dash of Latin and country to the proceedings, although not as much as it is used on the tunes he penned himself. The production is much cleaner and crisper than the version where Peter sings lead.

There is some cool prominent organ here that shows up quite a bit on these tracks. The blend of Mike singing harmony to Micky is always astounding, and Mike even gets the last line of the song to himself as Micky drops out for no explicable reason. There is also a hi-hat pattern in the drums that gets recycled on a few of these tracks as well. While producing tracks written by Goffin & King may not be as natural for Mike as producing his own, he acquits himself admirably here. While he was certainly thinking outside the box, Mike was not so experimental as to be unpalatable to the young listeners and I think the Powers-That-Be should've trusted him sooner to do more (if not all) of the production work on the debut record.

While Mike does a fine job with "I Don't Think You Know Me", clearly songs such as **"Papa Gene's Blues"** are where he feels most comfortable. Both the Latin and country elements are cranked up. The title is an unexplained inside joke that is not referred to in the lyrics in anyway. Mike was still trying to meet Kirshner halfway by writing about teen love, but that seems to be the only concession to convention made here. The lyrics are not condescending as so much pop music can be. The whole sound is visionary without being avant garde. Mike sounds like he knows how good this is and is having a grand old time singing it, letting loose with a "Yee-haw!" and even a somewhat cryptic "pick it, Luther!" (Mike was referring to Luther Perkins, Johnny Cash's longtime guitar player; although he may also be making an early jab at the fact the Monkees weren't playing their own instruments). The tune is lovely and holds up as well if not better than most of the Monkees' greatest hits. It's no surprise that when Mike tours solo that this is one of the few (if not only) Monkees tunes he throws into the set. But when the Monkees reunite - even without Mike, this song is frequently played as well. It's as close to a standard as Nesmith has ever written.

While Mike had produced two songs that could be considered Micky lead vocals at this point, they both felt like they could have (or were) sung by Mike. However, **"So Goes Love"** was definitely only meant for Davy to sing. This is another song written by Goffin & King. Of all the songwriters in Don Kirshner's stable, it was Goffin & King that Mike seemed particularly drawn to. While Mike has already played with the formula a bit, this song really digs into a lounge music/bossa nova territory.

Unfortunately, while this does not come off quite as successfully as the other tracks on this playlist, it is interesting to see where Mike though Davy fit into the whole Monkees sound. Clearly, Mike also thought that Davy should be singing the more romantic numbers to try and woo the hearts of teenage girls, but his way of going about it was a lot more circuitous. Davy does not seem to have taken this session any less seriously than those produced by professional outside record makers. It comes across okay, with some nice flamenco-ish guitar flourishes and cool electric piano playing, but it doesn't seem as committed or serious about the genre as later experiments like "Don't Call On Me" were. It is at least something different for Davy and a lot less mawkish than the tripe he usually had to peddle.

Mike seems to have cut back on his more idiosyncratic tendencies and tried to write a very straight-forward rock number with **"You Just May Be The One"**. When the Monkees re-recorded the tune with Chip Douglas for *Headquarters* they did manage to pull it off okay - including the somewhat tricky opening bass riff, but this version sounds a lot more confident and feels a lot smoother. The country guitar riffs have been minimized and only really come out during the bridge. The cowbell that propels the song is kept on a fairly standard quarter-note rhythm. Maybe Mike was just trying to prove to Kirshner that he could play the game and write actual pop music without having to resort to working with guys like Roger Atkins. Still Don Kirshner ended up passing on the track initially, although like "All The King's Horses" Bob & Bert felt no compunction about using the song in the TV show.

While Mike may have restrained himself on "You Just May Be The One" he goes all out on **"Sweet Young Thing"** and that song actually does get chosen for the first album. This was another one of Don Kirshner's forced play-dates with Mike co-writing the song with Goffin & King. While Mike did not like working with the two of them, he seems to really enjoy the song that they wrote together quite a bit.

This song is one of the most surreal experiments here; all pounding bass and crazy fiddle. It also has one of the best opening lines of any song ever "I know that something very strange has happened to my brain / I'm either feeling very good or else I am insane". This sets the stage for lyrics that are your typical "I love you" type affair - with some really strange metaphors and phrases thrown in. But it is the music itself that really stands out. It is relentless and throbbing, almost to the point of being hypnotic. While one would expect an unhinged vocal on top of this madness, Mike's delivery is calm, but still in awe of this wonderful girl. The guitar solo is reminiscent of the one that Boyce & Hart were doing at the time - rather than showing off in the front it is scratching away half-subliminally in the background. Micky's backing vocals become a chant reinforcing the almost cult-like effect the subject of the song has on its singer. I love the echo at the end of the solo section and the way it ends with Mike singing "thing-uh!" is perfect. This is one of Mike's best songs.

"I Won't Be The Same Without Her" is another Goffin & King song. Mike wasn't merely trying to placate the Powers-That-Be by recording so many tunes written by two of them. In 1969, long after the resignation of Kirshner, Mike went back re-recorded his vocals on this track for its inclusion on the *Instant Replay* album. It is a fairly standard rocker for this playlist with the same hi-hat pattern and country picking. The lyrics are unremarkable, but inoffensive musing on the loss of the love of a girl. The most interesting part is the "bah-da-bop-bop" backing vocals by Micky. While it is perfectly fine album filler, it certainly does not reach the heights of many of the tracks on this playlist. Intriguingly enough while Mike did produce a number of songs written by Goffin & King, Goffin & King did attempt to produce a version of Mike's "Carlisle Wheeling" in 1968 during the sessions for "Porpoise Song", "Look Down" and "As We Roll Along". As tantalizing as this cross-over may be, that version never got vocals overdubbed and has yet to see an official release.

While Mike didn't mind using the songwriting talents afforded him by working with Don Kirshner, he also wanted to help out and showcase some songs from his then-unknown friends as well. One of these friends was Michael Martin Murphey, who later went on to be a country singer in his own right. Before then, he wrote a couple of tunes for the Monkees including "Oklahoma Backroom Dancer" and "What Am I Doing Hangin' Round?" While those two country-ish tunes sound like his sort of style, **"(I Prithee) Do Not Ask For Love"** is a different beast altogether. The lyrical hook is the use of olde English pronouns and Biblical verb tenses. This song has been attempted several times by the Monkees. Peter recorded a very sparse version during *The Birds, The Bees, & The Monkees* sessions. Peter also sang a faux-Eastern flavored version on the ill-fated TV special *33 ⅓ Revolutions Per Monkee.*

While Peter kept trying to figure out how to make this song work, it was Mike who brought the piece to the Monkees project. His arrangement emphasizes the medieval conceit of the lyrics by using harpsichords and strings. Mike had both Davy and Micky attempt lead vocals here, and depending on how evenly you want to parse the lead vocals on the playlist either version works. To me, Davy feels like a better fit for the dramatic bent of the song than Micky, although it really is a bit of a toss-up.

Much like "So Goes Love", this song does feel a little at odds with the feel of the rest of the tracks on this playlist. While not horrible by any stretch, it's hard to see why Peter loved this song so much. The lyrics are a bit too arch and clever to really connect with the listener and the song never really explains why the singer is singing in such an archaic fashion. Is it supposed to be happening several centuries ago? Are his words supposed to be obeyed as if they were Bible verses? Is the narrator trying to say he feels like a peasant or serf? I'm not really sure.

Another friend of Michael's, Bill Martin, wrote **"Of You"**. This song is far less out-of-place than "(I Prithee) Do Not Ask For Love". While I love the overall feel and sound of the playlist, I will admit that sometimes the individual songs can be somewhat interchangeable and indistinct. The guitar solo is pure country and the organ is up nicely in the mix. The Latin percussion is once again evident. Ultimately, though this song feels a little like padding without as much invested in it as say "Papa Gene's Blues" or "Sweet Young Thing". Still it would've been a welcome addition to the Monkees' debut album.

While it may seem that **"Mary Mary"** was written by Mike with Micky's voice in mind, he actually sold the tune, pre-Monkees, to the Paul Butterfield Blues Band who recorded it on their *East-West* album. Still this doesn't seem to be a song Mike ever wanted to sing himself and there is no evidence of him singing it anywhere that I know of. This is easily the hardest rocking thing that Mike cut during this period. The maracas here are more Bo Didley than Latin. The country influence is almost completely absent here, although Mike complains that session guitarist Glen Campbell made the riff less bluesy and twangier than he had originally intended. I find this hard to believe as Glen Campbell was perfectly capable as a session musician of giving the producer what he wanted. He did not really become a country act until he broke out as a solo singer-songwriter on his own much later.

The Paul Butterfield version certainly does show off exactly how much of a blues tune this could be, but Mike is not primarily a blues writer. The lyrics, while still on the subject of romance, do have odd turns of phrases such as "this I'll vow ya" and "more than a clear thinking man would do" that make the song pure Nesmith. It would be great to hear Mike's vocals on this. I wonder how it would've changed it. Still Micky does a great job here, especially during the fade out when improvises on the titular name. A slight change of pace, this is a nifty little rock-number which would eventually become the basis for a hit for the rap group Run DMC. It is a fitting end for a productive month for Michael Nesmith. However he must've realized how futile his efforts were when the debut album came out with only two of his contributions on it. He must've seen the writing on the wall and known that he would have to first wrest control of the music away from Don Kirshner before he could really not only record, but release, his own vision for the Monkees.

MICHAEL NESMITH 2

1.) Carlisle Wheeling 3:20
(written by Michael Nesmith)
first released on *Missing Links Vol. I*
November 4th, 1967

2.) Tapioca Tundra 3:06
(written by Michael Nesmith)
from *The Birds, The Bees, & The Monkees*
November 11th, 1967

3.) Magnolia Simms 3:48
(written by Michael Nesmith and Charles Rockett)
from *The Birds, The Bees, & The Monkees*
December 2nd, 1967

4.) Writing Wrongs 5:09
(written by Michael Nesmith)
from *The Birds, The Bees, & The Monkees*
December 3rd, 1967

5.) Circle Sky 2:28
(written by Michael Nesmith)
from the soundtrack to *Head*
December 9th, 1967

6.) Auntie's Municipal Court 4:03
(written by Michael Nesmith and Keith Allison)
from *The Birds, The Bees, & The Monkees*
January 6th, 1968

7.) My Share of the Sidewalk 3:07
(written by Michael Nesmith)
first released on *Missing Links Vol. II*
January 9th, 1968

8.) Daddy's Song 2:27
(written by Harry Nilsson)
from the soundtrack to *Head*
January 10th, 1968

9.) Good Times
(written by Harry Nilsson)
from *Good Times!*
January 10th, 1968

10.) While I Cry 3:00
(written by Michael Nesmith)
first released on *Instant Replay*
January 14th, 1968

11.) War Games 2:13
(written by Davy Jones and Steve Pitts)
first released as a bonus track on *The Birds, The Bees, & The Monkees*
January 23rd, 1968

12.) Nine Times Blue 2:20
(written by Michael Nesmith)
first released as a bonus track on *The Birds, The Bees, & The Monkees*
February 8th, 1968

UNFINISHED SONGS FROM THESE SESSIONS:

Impack (written by Michael Nesmith)

Mr. Richland's Favorite Song (written by Harry Nilsson)

St. Matthew (written by Michael Nesmith)

Good Times (written by Harry Nilsson)

The Story Of Rock And Roll (written by Harry Nilsson)

Empire (written by Michael Nesmith)

Seasons (written by Michael Nesmith)

Produced by Michael Nesmith

MUSICIANS:
MICHAEL NESMITH: guitar, piano & organ
KEITH ALLISON & BILL CHADWICK: guitar
RICHARD DEY: bass
EDDIE HOH: drums
HARRY NILSSON: backing vocals (on "While I Cry"), keyboards (on "Auntie's Municipal Court"), piano and lead vocals (on "Good Times")
MICHEL RUBINI: piano (on "Daddy's Song")
JON ETHRIDGE: bass (on "Nine Times Blue")
JOE OSBORN: bass (on "War Games)
PETE CANDOLI, MARION CHILDERS & ANTHONY TERRAN: trumpet (on "Daddy's Song" and "My Share Of The Sidewalk")
RICHARD LEITH: trombone (on "Daddy's Song" and "My Share Of The Sidewalk")

JUSTIN DiTULLIO, RAPHAEL KRAMER, EMMET SARGEANT & ELEANOR SLATKIN: cello
   (on "Daddy's Song" and "My Share Of The Sidewalk")
BRENDAN CAHILL: percussion (on "Daddy's Song")
PAUL T. SMITH: piano (on "Magnolia Simms")
MAX BENNETT: bass (on "Magnolia Simms")
EARL PALMER: drums (on "Magnolia Simms")
JIM HORN: sax (on "Magnolia Simms")
JACK NIMITZ: baritone sax (on "Magnolia Simms")
OLIVER MITCHELL & SHORTY ROGERS: trumpet (on "Magnolia Simms")
LEW McCREARY: trombone (on "Magnolia Simms", "Daddy's Song" and "My Share Of The
   Sidewalk")
JUSTIN DiTULLIO, RAPHAEL KRAMER, EMMET SARGEANT & ELEANOR SLATKIN: cello
   (on "My Share Of The Sidewalk")
PETER TORK: banjo (on "Carlisle Wheeling")

Recorded 11/4/67 – 2/8/68

Once the cast of the Monkees stopped trying to work together and each went their own way, Michael went right back to producing tracks for the whole group. Maybe Mike thought he would finally get the chance to produce an entire Monkees' album that he was denied when Boyce & Hart's superseded Mike's songs for the debut album. He produced as many tunes sung by Davy as he did for himself; however he did hedge his bets by recording his own vocals for most of those tunes so that they could be swapped out if someone else was going to take care of cutting tracks for the other three Monkees. One of the oddest recordings from these sessions is a version of "Mr. Richland's Favorite Song" produced by Michael Nesmith with the same session musicians, but sung by its author, Harry Nilsson. It's uncertain if this was recorded for Harry as a demo or one of his albums; or if this was meant to have one of the Monkees come in and replace Harry's vocals. It seems like something Davy could've done well, but I would like to have heard Micky's vocals on top of this version.

This time around the country and Latin influences are muted a bit compared to the first Michael Nesmith playlist. However we do get a whole new ingredient added to the mix: 1920s jazz/ragtime. There are three songs on this playlist that really play it up: "Daddy's Song", "Magnolia Simms", and "My Share Of The Sidewalk". If these were released together with some of the songs that Micky was singing at the time, "D.W. Washburn", "I Didn't Know You Had It In You Sally", "Shake It Up" and "Don't Say Nothin'", plus a couple others of that ilk it certainly would've been a shock to Monkees fans at the time. It would've certainly delighted fans of The New Vaudeville Band's "Winchester Cathedral" however. I'm not sure if it was a coincidence or a deliberate decision that there were so many songs in this vein being recorded at that time. The failure of the "D.W. Washburn" single certainly stopped any further exploration in this particular direction from being released.

One thing that is notable in this playlist is the number of tunes that

Mike produced for Davy – even including one that Davy wrote. It is often assumed that in the Monkees spectrum that Mike was at one end and Davy was at the other. However, Mike actually seems for more able to use Davy as a vocalist now than he did on his first batch of songs. Meanwhile Micky's lead vocals are notably absent from this set.

As usual, Mike has no interest in bringing in Peter as a lead vocalist -- but did again tap him for his instrumental prowess. Although Peter didn't get to play banjo on "What Am I Doin' Hangin' 'Round?" he does get to shine on this version of **"Carlisle Wheeling"**. While the previous Nesmith playlist featured a subtle integration of his country influences, Mike now seems more interested in separating them out into songs that purely country and songs that don't have any twang in them. While the schism is not quite as drastic as it is on the next two playlists, "Carlisle Wheeling" is certainly one that belongs in the "definitely country" category. This is a song that Nesmith had some trouble with – even just the title. After this version he tried re-recording it later. Neither of those two vocal versions were released at the time, although an instrumental arrangement did come out on *The Wichita Train Whistle Sings* with the expanded title "Carlisle Wheeling Effervescent Popsicle". The song was eventually retitled as the less interesting "Conversations" when it finally did get released in yet another arrangement on the First National band's *Loose Salute*. Frankly, I think the version here with Peter's banjo and the prominent organ played by Mike is the best version (while the officially released version might be the weakest). The lyrics are a meditation on a love affair that is deepening but also becoming less intense. It's a great idea for a song, however the effectiveness of the lyrics gets a bit tangled up in an overly extended metaphor. Still the melody is lovely and it is a shame that it seems that Michael was never able to capture it to his satisfaction.

While the lyrical construct of "Carlisle Wheeling" may have undercut the song's simple message, the indecipherable words of **"Tapioca Tundra"** are less of an obstacle as the meaning of the lyrics is never made clear. This song is definitely odd duck. The lyrics are a trippy poem alá "Daily Nightly" and the music has some shades of both Latin and country, but mostly it is some sort of Byrds-style 12-string guitar psychedelic folk-rock feel. The long, protracted whistled intro, replete with countdown, does tend to scare off most people - but once the song kicks in, it's really pretty straight-forward if somewhat meaningless. The "solo" section is pretty weird too. Instead of a guitar or some other instrument taking the lead, you just get Mike singing "nyet" over and over while drenched in reverb. That may sound unlistenable, but it is actually pretty cool. This song is Mike's first lead vocal appearance on a Monkees' single, being the b-side to "Valleri". I'm not sure what Lester Sill was thinking when he picked this to be on the flipside. As great as "Tapioca Tundra" is, it is almost stubbornly anti-commercial. Maybe Lester figured it didn't really matter what the song was, since it was only a b-side. Plus it was in his best interest to keep Mike on his good side. While I could do without the weird intro myself, this is one of my all-time favorite Monkees' tracks.

Weird in a much more consistent way is the roaring 20s pastiche **"Magnolia Simms"**. In order to replicate the vintage mono of time period Mike put all of the sound into just one channel, making the song a little difficult to enjoy on headphones, if not downright alarming. To further complete the old-timey illusion, Michael added surface noise from a 78 rpm record and even has the track get stuck in the groove towards the end, only to hear the sound of the needle being moved and the song resuming. This recording is completely devoted to maintaining the facade. Most listeners find these additions distracting from the song itself, which is a cute little tune with a hummable melody and quaint gibberish lyrics. Personally I love Michael's commitment here and actually enjoy the sonic experiments of the recording. While there are mixes out there in stereo (or at least mono in both ears) and without all the sound effects for those who want to just listen to the song, I find the track to be weaker without them.

Michael clearly was enjoying his newly found freedom to experiment with the next track, **"Writing Wrongs"**. Many Monkees fans disparage the inclusion of this track on *The Birds, The Bees, & The Monkees*, while there are no Peter Tork numbers, making it seem even more self-indulgent than it is. It can be especially maddening considering that in the five minutes that this song takes you could've had "Alvin", "Merry-Go-Round", and "Seeger's Theme" and an extra two minutes for something like "Lady's Baby". But putting that aside, "Writing Wrongs" is a brave, fantastic, and fascinating track. It can be a bit difficult to listen to, but I think it's worth it.

The first third of the song is a nearly glacially paced, piano driven, rock song with lyrics that might mean something to Mike (or whomever Bill Chambers is) but don't mean anything to the average listener. While that would be challenging enough, it then breaks into a very long and much faster section of random noodling that feels spliced in from a completely different recording. It's all on various pianos and organs played by someone (probably Mike) who really isn't much of a keyboardist. So phrases get started and don't quite resolve, but then are repeated over and over again. This weirdness goes on for quite some time, never really reaching a conclusion, when the instrumental solo (or whatever you want to call it) suddenly stops and the first part of the song reinstates itself; giving us one last verse before trailing out. It is as weird as it sounds. I have heard fan edits of the song that take the middle part out, and in process nearly halve its running time. However, doing this makes the track very monochromatic and dull. It's only through listening to all these various keyboard lines trying (and failing) to get back to their tonal center that you can truly appreciate how unsettling this track is. Maybe not a masterpiece by any stretch, and you do definitely have to be in the mood for it, but "Writing Wrongs" has its charms.

After that extended bit of weirdness comes Mike's most straightforward balls-to-the-wall rocker, other than possibly "Mary Mary", the splendid **"Circle Sky"**. Once again the lyrics are pretty much meaningless, but since the vocals are so buried in the mix it almost doesn't matter anyway. The song was written to be performed live by the Monkees in the film *Head* and as such is deliberately pretty simple. Still the studio version, which most people (notably Peter Tork) find inferior to the live film version, is pretty amazing. Mostly bashing away on a single chord with long held vocal notes, the song creates incredibly tension that is somehow both relieved and ratcheted up by the chromatic descending chords that punctuate the song. It's hard to tell if the singer is frustrated or thankful to find that he has "made it once again" in the choruses, but either way the circular motif lets us know that he will soon be back where he started. This is a great song and it's a shame that Mike didn't do more of this proto-punk style rock songs either with the Monkees or on his own.

While Mike has plenty of songs on this playlist for Davy to sing, the only track Micky sings lead on, **"Auntie's Municipal Court"**, has Mike's harmony vocal turned up so loud in the mix that it almost comes across as a single-hybrid voice, much like "All The King's Horses". This song falls somewhere between the experimentalism of "Tapioca Tundra" and the simplicity of "Circle Sky." I'm not quite sure why Michael needed the help of Keith Allison, session guitarist and member of Paul Revere & The Raiders, to write this song as it is simply a I-IV-V jam over a single repeated guitar riff. The lyrics are pretty incomprehensible, although the line "It used to come as one now it comes as four" could refer to the way that Monkees' music was no longer going to be the product of all four Monkees unified under Chip Douglas, but each working on their own. Ultimately, the song fails to be strange enough to be memorable, but isn't strong enough to work as a simple rock tune either and ends up being one of the weaker tracks on this playlist.

"My Share Of The Sidewalk" is in fact one of the strangest tunes Mike ever wrote, but tries to be a straight-ahead broadway-esque song for Davy to sing. While the chords and pretty standard for a Nesmith composition, the time signature changes are all over the map and show either a real sophistication or willful ignorance when it comes to music theory. 5/4, 6/8 and 7/4 are all competing in varying measures with your standard rock 4/4. Davy does an impressive job managing the tricky corners of the song, making it sound so effortless that you might not notice how weird the rhythmic structure of the song is. The lyrics are ostensibly about a girl the singer likes and as such are a bit more straightforward than some of the songs on this playlist, but do contain some very weird turns of phrase. Shorty Roger's horn arrangement makes the whole thing seem a lot less complicated than it is, and I almost prefer the demo version with Mike singing and playing the piano because it throws these musical oddities into a more stark relief.

With "My Share Of The Sidewalk", Mike seems to have finally cracked the code of what to give Davy to sing that fits him well but isn't his standard goopy fare. Mike did go back to this song later and record a version that didn't have vocals (by either Davy or himself) that straightens and flattens out some of the more weird meter changes on this song, making it far less interesting - although using strings, marimba, and pedal steel still makes this quite the production. This instrumental backing track became the basis for the version recorded (but also left unreleased) by the obscure group, P.K. Ltd. That take is worth hunting down and listening to if you can, but Davy's vocal version simply blows it away and this is another one of my all-time favorite Monkees tracks.

A far more conventional Davy tune, **"Daddy's Song"** is another jaunty 1920s music hall type of song. Like "Cuddly Toy" this song was penned by Harry Nilsson, one of the best writers of this type of music. While this song may seem to be quintessentially Davy, there is a version out there with Mike's vocals on top of it instead. In Mike's hands the song becomes something of a winking homage to the time period, sort of like "Magnolia Simms" but not as strong. Davy however treats this song as contemporary and therefore helps sell it a bit better. This tune seems specifically to be designed as a dance showcase for Davy, which it pretty much was in the film *Head*. Still Michael's production here shows his genuine fondness for this type of material and they pull it off splendidly. No one would ever mistake it for an actual recording or even composition from that time period, but everyone involved imbues it with the same feel and color as those old ragtime pieces.

While Harry Nilsson is a very talented man with a lot of different talents, one thing he was not really known for is rocking out. This makes the song **"Good Times"** something of an anomaly. Harry is really trying to right a straight-forward hard-rocking song here. Another thing that Nilsson is not known for is turning in a half-hearted performance. This is god because even though this song was originally cut in 1968 with Harry's voice as a guide vocal, he turned in such a stellar performance that when this track was dusted off for the *Good Times!* album, Micky was album to turn this song into a duet with his departed friend. Even though this track isn't as hard or heavy as it sounds like it's trying to be, it is just as catchy or fun as anything else that Harry penned for The Monkees. Plus it is great to hear Micky singing on another song within this playlist.

Harry Nilsson also does some backing vocals on **"While I Cry"**, but this is a very straight-ahead country tune, much like "Carlisle Wheeling". Although with the lack of fiddles, banjos, or pedal steel guitars, one could argue this was more "acoustic rock" than it was actual country music. The romantic lyrics are not hidden in any weird allegories and the language is pretty plain-spoken. The theme is once again that the woman in question may not be who she says she is.

Mike was clearly starting to create a dividing line between these two types of songs: the experimental and the pop. And yet his pop is going country - which at the time was still considered pretty anti-commercial. While the melody is almost heartbreaking and the playing on it is sincere, the overall track tends to be forgotten as Mike would later do a lot of this kind of stuff, and usually as well if not better. Still it is nice to see that Mike was able to switch back and forth between these two increasingly disparate sides of his personality, while not appearing to be schizophrenic.

It is a statement to Michael's commitment to recording music for the rest of the Monkees that he actually produced a version of the song **"War Games"** that was not only sung, but written, by Davy. The song was composed by Davy and his co-writer Steve Pitts for the movie *Head* which may be why Mike was willing to work on it. However Nesmith doesn't seem terribly interested in the tune either. He doesn't add or embellish anything here; he just gives it a pretty straight-forward kind of fast rock production with some country-ish picking on the lead guitar.

It is not all that surprising that he didn't do more, since "War Games" is very slight song. Davy was not much of a songwriter at this point. The lyrics, which were meant to be topical anti-war stuff, feel very dated now. The music is very basic, still Mike is respectful and does a good job. Although not good enough for Davy, who a short time later produced a version that was much slower and more pompous with lots of strings on top. Either way, not a great song, but of the two this is the better version.

Mike also produced a version of **"Nine Times Blue"** for Davy to sing. The song's country (or acoustic rock) feel seems tailor-made for Mike's vocals and has later become one of his signature tracks, being the second song on his first post-Monkees album *Magnetic South*. So it is a bit of a shock the first time you hear Davy's English voice on it. Mike did also record his own vocals for this version of the song, but I always preferred Davy's take and not just for the sake of sharing the lead vocals more evenly on this playlist. As anyone who's heard Ringo Starr's solo album *Beaucoups Of Blues* or Elvis Costello's *Almost Blue* can attest, the combination of a British accent on the traditional country sound can be very appealing.

Soon Mike would give up on recording songs for the rest of the Monkees to sing, so it is nice to get one last glimpse of him trying to find a way to meld his peculiar interests with the expectations of a "pop" group and the skills of the rest of his cast mates. However, Michael was now moving even further into an undeniably country sound and it may have been that the rest of the group simply felt uncomfortable in what was clearly Nesmith's bailiwick.

MICHAEL NESMITH 3

1.)   Nine Times Blue 2:10
(written by Michael Nesmith)
first released on *Missing Links Vol. I*
April 5th, 1968

2.)   Carlisle Wheeling 3:12
(written by Michael Nesmith)
first released as a bonus track on *Instant Replay*
April 5th, 1968

3.)   Propinquity 3:21
(written by Michael Nesmith)
first released on *Missing Links Vol. III*
May 28th, 1968

4.)   Don't Wait For Me 2:35
(written by Michael Nesmith)
from *Instant Replay*
May 29th, 1968

5.)   Some Of Shelly's Blues 2:33
(written by Michael Nesmith)
first released on *Missing Links Vol. II*
May 29th, 1968

6.)   The Crippled Lion 2:52
(written by Michael Nesmith)
first released on *Missing Links Vol. II*
May 29th, 1968

7.)   Hollywood 2:17
(written by Michael Nesmith)
first released on *Missing Links Vol. III*
May 31st, 1968

8.) How Insensitive 2:33
(written by Antonio Carlos Jobim, Vinicus DeMoraes, and Norman Gimbel)
first released on *Missing Links Vol. III*
May 31st, 1968

9.) Listen To The Band 2:43
(written by Michael Nesmith)
first released on *The Monkees Present*
June 1st, 1968

10.) Good Clean Fun 2:19
(written by Michael Nesmith)
first released on *The Monkees Present*
June 1st, 1968

11.) St. Matthew 2:44
(written by Michael Nesmith)
first released on *Missing Links Vol. II*
June 2nd, 1968

Produced by Michael Nesmith

MUSICIANS:
DAVID BRIGGS, LARRY BUTLER: organ, piano
KENNY BUTTREY, WILLIE ACKERMAN, JERRY CARRIGAN:
   drums
LLOYD GREEN: pedal steel guitar
WAYNE MOSS, HAROLD BRADLEY, BILLY SANFORD: guitar
SONNY OSBORNE, BOBBY THOMPSON: banjo
NORBERT PUTNAM, BOBBY DYSON: bass
BUDDY SPICHER: fiddle
CHARLIE McCOY: harmonica
CHIP DOUGLAS: bass (on "Carlisle Wheeling" and "Nine Times Blues")
ORVILLE "RED" RHODES: pedal steel guitar (on "Carlisle Wheeling" and "Nine Times Blues")
MICHAEL NESMITH: guitar (on "Carlisle Wheeling" and "Nine Times Blues")

Recorded 4/5/68 and 5/28/86 – 6/2/68

These are the now infamous Nashville sessions. It's hard to tell exactly what Mike's intentions were for these sessions. It seems that Mike had given up on producing an entire album for the Monkees and concentrated just on tunes for himself as no one else sang on any of these tracks. Was this going to be a solo album; and if so how did he expect to release it while still under contract with the Monkees? (He did manage to sneak out *The Wichita Train Whistle Sings* by not singing or putting his name on it, but just producing it). Did he expect the songs to be cherry-picked and put onto other albums (which was what ended up happening)? Did he worry, or even care, that these tracks would not fit into any sort of consistent sound for the Monkees? Or did he just do what he wanted because he could and not really think at all about what was going to happen to these recordings after he was done with them?

With only nine tracks recorded it's almost, but not quite, enough for a solo album. Maybe that's why he did re-do two of the more country tunes from the last playlist less than two months before he went to Nashville. These two tracks were recorded in a very similar style, so maybe they were meant to be mixed into this theoretical solo album. It certainly feels like a dry run at the solo career that Michael was about to start in two years as seven of the eleven tunes on this playlist were later re-recorded and released with either the First National Band or solo in the seventies. Although only three of these did show up on official Monkees' releases at the time, the Monkees (now a trio) did sing a superb version of "Nine Times Blue" live on the "Johnny Cash Show" in 1969, in what would be an attempt to promote the sales of a record that didn't see release by the Monkees until nearly 20 years later.

Despite all of the uncertain motivations however, this playlist does make for one of the more consistent listens in this book, albeit one that seems to have the least to do with popular image of the Monkees as it existed at the time. While it may be consistent, whether or not you actually enjoy these songs depends a lot on your feelings about the sound of country music in general. While previous ventures into this territory merely added a bit of twang to what was already an existing pop-rock style, these tunes make almost no concessions to the prevailing sounds of the times. It is often credited as being part of the birth of country-rock, but the sessions have very little of the rock half of the equation left in them. At least to my ears. Maybe someone a little more well-versed in the country music world would be see these track as obvious outliers of the real country music sound. While these tunes may be very straight-forward country musically, lyrically they do tend to be a lot more intricate and complex.

The first two non-Nashville track cuts here have a couple of things in common. First, they were both recorded without any drums. Secondly, both are attempts at re-recording tunes that Michael had tried earlier on the previous playlist when he was still interested in trying to produce a Monkees sound that included the other three members. For these tracks he is clearly going out on his own. The version of **"Nine Times Blue"** is much closer to the sound on the First National Band record that everyone is familiar with than it is to the take that was sung by Davy. It is still a great song with a wonderful lyrics and a truly sensitive vocal turn by Mike. The First National Band version suffers from having a second whispered vocal by Mike that is both creepy and distracting. This version is much more palatable although not nearly as interesting or adventurous as having Davy sing it.

"Carlisle Wheeling" was sung by Mike on both versions, but the difference between these two is pretty telling. Mike seemed to be merely flirting with country on the previous incarnation, while here he seems to have accepted it. While Peter's banjo on the previous could've tipped that take into a more Nashville sound, it instead comes across as more of a folk-flavoring on top of a pop-rock song especially with the prominent organ. On the second version, the pedal steel guitar erases any illusion that the tune was ever meant to be anything but country-and-western. The first version is also a little bit peppier in tempo which I think helps the track a lot, as the second version tends to drag. By the time it is finally released on *Loose Salute* as "Conversations" the song is practically lethargic. While the starts and stops in the First National Band version are a nice addition, with each succeeding revision of the tune Mike seems to have gotten further away from the goal of this song.

The first track that Mike did attempt in Nashville with his studio vets was **"Propinquity"**, a tune that, despite its odd title, had been floating around pre-Monkees. There is a great demo version with just Mike on acoustic guitar and John London on upright bass that was released as a bonus track on one of the deluxe re-issues of the Monkees' self-titled debut. I will frequently include that track when I am listening to the first Michael Nesmith playlist as I love it so much - however I doubt it was ever intended for public consumption and therefore did not include it there in this book.

While that version of the song could be a John Denver-style folk song, here we get the full-blast of Michael was intending in Nashville; and that is country with a capital C. It is a great melody and wonderful lyrics about suddenly seeing the woman whom he had overlooked before. While it is one of Mike's best tunes, it is no surprise that when Lester Sill passed on releasing this recording on any of the Monkees albums. Mike did eventually get this song released with the First National Band for their third and final album, *Nevada Fighter*. That version of the song is beautiful and pristine and generally benefits from a more stripped down production. The Nashville arrangement of "Propinquity" tends to overwhelm the lovely little melody a bit, making one have to work a little harder to uncover it from the layers of instrumentation. The "Monkees" take also has a slightly faster tempo which I think undercuts the more reflective mood of the song. Still, a song like this shines through almost no matter who does it or how well they do it. Plus, the title will teach you a new vocabulary word (it means nearness).

While "Propinquity" may have been underserved by the Nashville sound, **"Don't Wait For Me"** seems almost like it was deliberately written to be a generic country-and-western song. The lyrics are the typical tearful "woe is me" that the genre specializes in. There is nothing about this song that seems particularly Monkees - or even like it was especially Nesmith, which makes it odd that this is one of the tracks that actually did see release at the time. It seems unlikely that the track would've drawn previously hardcore country fans into the Monkees fold, nor does it make any concessions to current Monkees fans to try and ease them into the world of country music. Not only that, but is one of the weaker and less interesting songs that Mike wrote or recorded during this period; nothing really wrong with it, but compared to some of his other stuff it's completely forgettable.

With a title that makes it seem like a sequel to "Papa Gene's Blues", **"Some Of Shelly's Blues"** is more like "Don't Wait For Me" but much better. The lyrics aren't nearly as tame and the melody is much catchier. Still this tune didn't seem to have stuck in Mike's craw the way some of the others did. While a lot of these songs were redone for Mike's first three solo albums, this one had to wait till his sixth solo album, *Pretty Much Your Standard Ranch Stash*. Even then, the Nitty Gritty Dirty Band had already had a minor hit with this song before then on their 1970 album *Uncle Charlie & His Dog Teddy*. This version might have assuaged his need to record it right away after leaving the Monkees, although its popularity may have finally encouraged him to release his own version. It's perfectly fine number, both the Nashville recording and the solo version, and it has become one of Michael's standards, but there's not much to say about this one either.

While the lyrics to "Some Of Shelly's Blues" are still centered on romantic boy-girl relationships, the title and words to **"The Crippled Lion"** are a bit more esoteric. This is a somewhat pretentious song, although clearly Mike felt the need to get this tune out there right away, re-recording it for the first of his post-Monkees releases. Both versions are cut at a dragging tempo. Other than the cosmic-cowboy nature of the lyrics, this sounds like a by-the-numbers country tune.

While the lyrics to **"Hollywood"** are typically inscrutable, the title would lead one to believe that this is a song about Michael's experience with the Monkees. However the tune was written prior to the Monkees, so who knows what it's really about. Like so many of the tracks here, it was later re-recorded by the First National Band. The Nashville version is pretty standard fare for the songs on this playlist. The version released on *Magnetic South* however, is a long trippy take. It's not even the slower tempo that extends the song's length so much as a psychedelic break-down and jam section that takes the song from under two and a half minutes to over five minutes. The longer version is kind of cool at first but eventually starts to get boring. Still, that's better than the Nashville version, which never rises to level of interesting.

With the strict adherence to the country sound, this playlist does tend to get a little monochromatic. Not only are the more pop/rock overtones lost, but we see very little of the Latin flavor that Mike used to use on his recordings. This omission becomes more obvious with the sole cover on this playlist, the bossa nova classic **"How Insensitive"** by Antonio Carlos Jobim. Normally, this song would be a perfect opportunity for Mike to break out the maracas and cowbells, but instead he sticks to his guns with the instrumentation. The result is a very weird and singular hybrid; which flourishes in this environment for being so different. However, once you get used to it, it is quite enjoyable and it makes one wish that Mike - or somebody - had really explored a full country-bossa nova cross-over. Although Mike does come back to this combination in a slight way for his 1992 album, *Tropical Campfires*, which instead of a traditional drum kit only feature Louis Conte's Latin percussion. Although it is a cover, this is my favorite track from this particular playlist.

Second only to "Papa Gene's Blues", Mike's most well-known contribution to the Monkees' catalogue is **"Listen To The Band"**. It's kind of an odd choice on some levels. There's not much to the song: only verse that is repeated as often as needed, no real chorus, just frequent instrumental breaks that are ideal in a live setting for letting each member of the backing band get introduced and take a short solo. That may be part of the reason why it has been a staple of Mike's solo concert act as well as appearing regularly on the various Monkees set-lists even when Mike wasn't joining in. The first glimpse the public had of the tune is on the TV special *33⅓ Revolutions Per Monkee* when the four Monkees played it live together by themselves. Despite the shoddy audio quality of the entire special, this is a great version, at least until the entire cast and crew glom on to the song turning it into an interminable freak-out. Despite the fact this song was released under the Monkees' name and as a single, Mike did go back and re-record it with the First National Band. That version emphasizes how slight the song is as a composition. Although both fading it in and fading it out gives one the weird feeling that the First National Band had been playing the song forever - or at least for hours. Otherwise the version on *Loose Salute* is completely unnecessary.

Really, the Nashville version is the one that really makes the song seem special. The chords are basically the same as "Nine Times Blue" played backwards and the inconsequential lyrics are just an excuse to have something to sing. Mike has relented on the strict country feel and put some out-of-character R&B horns on top of the C&W Nashville cats. After running through the only lyric enough times for people to get the gist, the tune stops and turns into the organ part from "The Porpoise Song". From there the drums fade back in and the song resumes briefly before being consumed by the sound of the screaming fans at a Monkees concert. Strip away these wild inventions, and there's not much going on here. But Mike has turned this small framework of a song into a monster of a record.

"Good Clean Fun" is a far more standard country tune, but it comes off much better than a lot of the tunes here. The feel is definitely a very Tennessee Two "boom-chicka" sound. The lyrics are once again plain and understandable; although the title was added on as an inside insult to someone at Mike's publishing company who told him that he had to put the title of his songs into the actual lyric. When "Listen To The Band" became a surprise mild success, this track was released as a single, but did not fare nearly as well. Since it was released by the Monkees, this is not a track that Mike really came back to, although there is an interesting bootleg of Peter singing it at a late 80's Monkees reunion floating around out there. Otherwise, the song has been pretty much forgotten.

While much has been made of these sessions being important to the development of "country rock", the only song here that really rocks is **"St. Matthew"**. While played by Nashville session musicians, the song is centered around a strong electric guitar riff. The lyrics are again in the "Tapioca Tundra"/"Daily Nightly" territory, although apparently according to Mike they are about Bob Dylan and his use of biblical imagery on *the John Wesley Harding* album. I would definitely recommend using the version with the Leslie Organ speaker effect on the vocal as the whooshing exhalation Mike makes at the beginning of the song just sounds silly without it. This is one of the better tracks recorded at the time but was passed over by Lester Sill. Unlike the rest of those songs, Mike never did go back to this song as a solo artist and the track remained unreleased until it appeared on the Monkees rarities compilation, *Missing Links Vol. II*.

It seems that the Powers-That-Be were far more interested in finding songs with words that make sense like "Good Clean Fun" and "Don't Wait For Me" to release rather than using the tracks that were the best to listen to. It did however leave Mike plenty of stuff to work with when he did break out on his own as a solo artist. Only one song on the first side of the first album by the First National Band wasn't first attempted during Mike's tenure with the Monkees. That track was "Joanne", one of only three new songs that Mike wrote for *Magnetic South*. While not a huge hit, "Joanne" was the biggest success of Michael's solo career in terms of record sales.

MICHAEL NESMITH 4

1.) Oklahoma Backroom Dancer 2:36
(written by Michael Martin Murphey)
from *The Monkees Present*
May 27th, 1969

2.) You're So Good 2:43
(written by Robert Stone)
first released on *Missing Links Vol. III*
May 27th, 1969

3.) Little Red Rider 3:18
(written by Michael Nesmith)
first released on *Missing Links Vol. III*
May 28th, 1969

4.) Calico Girlfriend Samba 2:33
(written by Michael Nesmith)
first released as a bonus track on *The Monkees Present*
May 29th, 1969

5.) Never Tell A Woman Yes 3:47
(written by Michael Nesmith)
from *The Monkees Present*
June 2nd, 1969

6.) Down The Highway 2:17
(written by Gerry Goffin and Carole King)
first released on *Missing Links Vol. II*
June 5th, 1969

7.) Angel Band 3:26
(written by William Bradbury and Jefferson Hascall)
first released on *Missing Links Vol. III*
June 9th, 1969

UNFINISHED SONGS FROM THESE SESSIONS:
Thirteen Is Not Our Lucky Number 2:40 (written by Michael Nesmith)
Lynn Harper 3:16 (written by Michael Nesmith)
Thank You My Friend 3:43 (written by Michael Nesmith)
Omega 2:16 (written by Michael Nesmith)
Good Afternoon 2:35 (author unknown)
A Bus That Never Comes 2:50 (written by Jack Keller and Bob Russell)
Till Then 3:19 (written by Eddie Seiler, Guy Wood, and Sol Marcus)
London Bridge 4:52 (written by David Gates)
Little Tommy Blues 3:53 (written by Tommy Griffin)
Michigan Blackhawk 2:55 (written by Michael Nesmith)

Produced by Michael Nesmith

MUSICIANS:
MICHAEL NESMITH: acoustic guitar
AL CASEY, MIKE DEASY, LOUIE SHELTON: guitar
MAX BENNETT & JOE OSBORN: bass
HAL BLAINE: drums
MICHAEL RUBINI & LARRY KNETCHEL: piano
JAMES BURTON: guitar (on "You're So Good")
BOB WEST: bass (on "You're So Good")
EDDIE HOH: drums (on "Oklahoma Backroom Dancer")
EARL PALMER: drums (on "You're So Good")
AL CASEY: banjo (on "Never Tell A Woman Yes")
CLIFFORD SOLOMON: tenor sax
MACK JOHNSON: trumpet
LESTER ROBERTSON: trombone

recorded 5/27/69 - 6/10/69

As muddled as motivation was for Michael's Nashville sessions were, the motivation for these tracks is even less clear. He did produce several track written by outside writers, including Goffin & King. He did end up recording the Micky-sung "You're So Good" as well as marking the tape box for "Calico Girlfriend Samba" for Davy. Mike only recorded vocals for about a third of the tracks done during these sessions. Perhaps Michael was thinking of having Davy and Micky (Peter had quit by this point) singing these and finally producing a whole Monkees' album himself. On the other hand, Mike was halfway out the Monkees door by this point and maybe he just wanted an excuse to spend someone else's corporate money on a bunch of musical experiments that required expensive session musicians, but didn't have any intentions of ever seeing the light of day.

Unlike the last set of sessions Mike recorded this is also one of the wildest and most varied, with R&B numbers, Tex-Mex stompers, faux-

Samba arrangements, doo-wop and other odd influences added to the mix. Given the highly instrumental and unfinished nature of most of these recordings, they are a lot harder to enjoy than the other three Michael Nesmith playlists, but they do conjure up a lot of "what if's. Generally, I avoided talking about unfinished instrumentals in this book, although there are some interesting ones like "Jokes", "All The Grey Haired Men", and "Where Has It All Gone?". The Monkees, understandably, never released any non-vocal tracks during the original run except for the track from the *Head* soundtrack's "Swami - Plus Strings" by Ken Thorne. I am guessing that all of these tunes were meant to have vocals on them at some point. However, since there are so many of them (ten!) I will briefly note how I can imagine some of these songs being performed had they been completed at the time.

It's a little easier to hypothesize with the cover songs because we know what the melody and lyrics are. It's a little tougher with the originals since we don't really know what they are supposed to sound like. Plus Mike's habit of giving his songs titles that aren't actually in the lyrics makes them even harder to decipher. I like to imagine the more up-tempo horn-driven tunes being sung by Micky since he was doing that whole R&B/Soul mash-up with Sam & The Goodtimers at the time. There are three Nesmith originals here that I think could fit in really well with Micky's vocals. There is the somewhat bluesy rock tune "Omega" which hopefully had an interesting melody to it because the backing track is nothing terribly special. Despite the somewhat bland title, "Lynn Harper" is a funky, horn-driven, soul number with an intro riff that sounds nearly identical to the one used by the Tork-less trio when they did "I'm A Believer" on the Joey Bishop show in 1969. I can definitely hear Micky singing the Chuck Berry-esque "Michigan Blackhawk".

The softer ballads I assume would be assigned to Davy, just because that's what Davy tends to do. There is "A Bus That Never Comes" which was also covered by Shirley Bassey around this time as the b-side of "Fa-Fa-Fa (Live For Today)". Her version is done in a much brassier style than this laid-back feeling of the backing track. The Nesmith original "Good Afternoon" is another song that almost falls into smooth jazz territory, especially the runs in the guitar break. "Thank You My Friend" is a waltz that Michael wrote in a similar vein which would seem to fit Davy's voice far more than "Calico Girlfriend Samba" would have. "London Bridge" was written by David Gates, who wrote "Saturday's Child" back on the first album. He was also at this time forming the extremely soft rock band Bread, who would record their own version of it. While all this wussiness would seem to make the track a natural Davy, Michael's production here is pretty weird and abstract with a long intro of what seems to be just noises made by the various instruments accompanied by a funereal drum pounding. It does get a little more straightforward eventually, but it is nothing like the bland Bread version.

Since this is purely hypothetical, I like to think that Peter may have come back for this theoretical album and Mike would have actually started to use him as a lead vocalist. "Thirteen Is Not Our Lucky Number" would be good for him to sing because it kind of sounded like a cross between "Your Auntie Grizelda" and "Tear The Top Right Off My Head". I know Nez actually wrote that song pre-Monkees and has recorded a demo (that I've not heard) during the early days as well as attempting it with the First National Band during the sessions for their first two albums. I would love to know what the lyrics and melody to this actually are. There is a great clip of Peter in 2011 singing the old Mills Brothers' tune "Till Then" on YouTube, so maybe he would've sung that here as well. It might also explain why Mike recorded a whole track of people chattering and laughing in the background of this song. Also, Peter's recent work with his band the Shoe Suede Blues leads one to think that he could've covered the Tommy Griffin tune "Little Tommy's Blues" although more likely Mike would've also had Micky in mind to sing that one.

The first song that Mike got around to actually recording vocals for, **"Oklahoma Backroom Dancer"** was written by his good friend Michael Martin Murphey. This is not country-rock as much as it is Southern Rock of the type that would be practiced by the Allman Brothers or Lynyrd Skynyrd. It's a simple three chord boogie-woogie with ridiculous lyrics praising some dancer. Frankly, it's kind of embarrassing and one hopes Mike only recorded out of loyalty to his friend. Of all the great material Mike had in the can though, this is one of the tracks that Lester Sill selected for inclusion on *The Monkees Present*. I'm not really sure why. It's pretty wooden in feel and ham-fisted in execution. Even my love for that album can't quite elevate this track in my mind.

After the near absence on the second Mike Nesmith playlist, it is nice to see that he was able to get a vocal out of Micky one last time. After Peter Tork's departure from the project, the Monkees needed a backing band in order to go on tour. For some inexplicable reason they chose Sam & The Goodtimers, the former backing band for Ike & Tina Turner. Almost no audio evidence of this tour exists, but from all accounts this odd combination of R&B horns on top of the Monkees sounded a lot like **"You're So Good"**. The song is not quite the same as "You're So Good To Me" from the album *Changes*, but close enough that Robert Stone is frequently credited as a co-writer on that tune as well.

The song is a pretty straight-forward soul number, and along with "Look Down", "Changes" and the version of "I'm A Believer" from *33 ⅓ Revolutions Per Monkee* all give something of an indication of what an entire Monkees concert or album in this style might've sounded like. It's not bad, but not very interesting either. The most annoying part is when Micky, who otherwise does a splendid job, sings "if you were a penny, you'd be good as good". He obviously misread the lyric sheet as it should've been "good as gold" which not only rhymes and also makes more sense in the context of the lyrics.

"Little Red Rider" is Michael's only written and sung entry into this more horn-infused style. For those who are only familiar with the song as the opening track on the First National Band's *Magnetic South*, this previously unheard arrangement can be a bit jarring. Frankly, I think it works better in this R&B setting than it does as a country-rock number. Listening to the solo acoustic demo, it's clear the song was pretty elastic and didn't have any set style affixed when it was originally written. The version here is funky, the guitar solo at the end is great, and there is some nifty cowbell playing buried down in the mix. It seems like Mike wasn't satisfied with this vision of the song and set it aside never to be revisited during his Monkees tenure.

While "Little Red Rider" is an attempt at soul music; **"Calico Girlfriend Samba"** is, as one would expect, a samba. This tune was also re-recorded in the more country manner by the First National Band. As much as I love those records, I appreciate the stylistic variety that Michael was getting with the tunes on this playlist. Granted, he had a larger budget and wasn't constrained to the same four musicians so he was able to vary his approach more under the Monkees' production banner. Mike clearly seems to be having a good time here mumbling about corn silk at the beginning and ad-libbing about Carmen Miranda in Rhode Island at the end. For all the Latin sensibilities that Mike had toyed with in his previous productions, this is the only song that fully committed itself to that sound. A whole samba album by Mike might be a bit much to take, but it would be fun to hear him try.

"Never Tell A Woman Yes" brings Mike back to the ragtime pastiche of "Magnolia Simms" and "Daddy's Song" only with a dash more southern rock sprinkled on top. The lyrics are some of the most comprehensible Mike has ever written. It tells a simple story of earning the love of a woman by not robbing her. It's hard to say exactly what the moral of this story is; it seems to be a positive message about not being materialistic and not judging someone simply by their wealth, but it gets a little confused. It's not a great song by any stretch, and it does tend to run a little long in order to get the plot of the story out. It does, however, end with a great little bit with Mike vocalizing in the style of each instrument as it takes a short solo break. This is the kind of thing that Harry Nilsson did much better.

After a long break from covering songs written by Goffin & King, Mike is back with **"Down The Highway"**. This song suffered the ignobility of being mistakenly titled "Michigan Blackhawk" and credited to Nesmith when it was finally released on *Missing Links Vol. II*. The song itself is another up-tempo boogie-woogie, which is actually much better than "Oklahoma Backroom Dancer" which did get released. Still there's not much to the song; although it's interesting the way that the length of each line of the verse varies. The production is pretty much nondescript southern rock. The lyrics seem quasi-meaningful and therefore tailor-made for Mike. After the genre experiments of "Calico Girlfriend Samba" and "Little Red Rider" this is a little disappointing.

"Angel Band" on the other hand is nothing but a genre exercise. While it is hard to say what the exact amount of devotion Michael has to the Christian Science beliefs of his upbringing, I can't imagine that this song was recorded with the sincere intent of proselytizing. Instead this is a very real attempt at capturing the sound and the mood of protestant hymn. This is not gospel music and sounds almost deliberately square and amateurish, as if one were overhearing an actual church service is a small town. The organ is chummy and the choir is well-intentioned but unprofessional. As skillful as the song is at creating an illusion, it is not all that fun to listen to very often. While Bob Dylan's born again era albums are still palatable to the non-believer audience simply by being so heartfelt, the confusing lack of intent here makes this faux-hymn harder to swallow. Still, it is again nice to see Michael trying out new styles and seeing what works and what doesn't, something he doesn't do nearly enough in his solo career, which was about to begin pretty shortly after these tracks were recorded.

DAVY JONES 1

1.) The Girl I Left Behind Me / A Girl Named Love 4:32
(written by Neil Sedaka & Carole Bayer / written by Davy Jones and Charlie Smalls)
first released as a bonus track on *The Birds, The Bees, & The Monkees*
October 31st, 1967

2.) Ceiling In My Room 3:50
(written by Davy Jones, Don DeMieri, and Robert Dick)
first released as a bonus track on *The Birds, The Bees, & The Monkees*
November 14th, 1967

3.) War Games 2:34
(written by Davy Jones and Steve Pitts)
first released on *Missing Links Vol. I*
February 6th, 1968

4.) Dream World 3:21
(written by Davy Jones and Steve Pitts)
from *The Birds, The Bees, & The Monkees*
February 6th, 1968

5.) Changes 2:28
(written by Davy Jones and Steve Pitts)
first released on *Missing Links Vol. II*
February 6th, 1968

6.) We Were Made For Each Other 2:25
(written by Carole Bayer and George Fischoff)
from *The Birds, The Bees, & The Monkees*
February 6th, 1968

7.) It's Nice To Be With You 2:54
(written by Jerry Goldstein)
released as the b-side of the "D.W. Washburn Single" single
February 6th, 1968

8.) The Poster 2:21
(written by Davy Jones and Steve Pitts)
from *"The Birds, The Bees, & The Monkees"*
February 15th, 1968

9.) I'm Gonna Try 2:44
(written by Davy Jones and Steve Pitts)
first released as a bonus track on *The Birds, The Bees, & The Monkees*
February 15th, 1968

10.) The Party 3:02
(written by Davy Jones and Steve Pitts)
first released on *Missing Links Vol. I*
February 15th, 1968

Produced by Davy Jones

MUSICIANS:
JAMES BURTON, AL CASEY, MICHAEL DEASY, AL
    HENDRICKSON, GERRY McGEE, & HOWARD ROBERTS: guitar
MAX BENNETT & LYLE RITZ: bass
DON RANDI & MICHAEL MELVOIN: piano, harpsichord, organ
EARL PALMER & HAL BLAINE: drums
BRENDAN CAHILL, GARY COLEMAN, GENE ESTES, TERESA HELFER, MILT HOLLAND
    & JERRY WILLIAMS: percussion
SAM FREED, NATHAN KAPROFF, GEORGE KAST, MARVIN LIMONICK, ALEXANDER
    MURRAY, ERNO NEUFELD & AMBROSE RUSSO: violin
MARIE FERA, EDGAR LUSTGARTEN, JACQUELINE LUSTGARTEN, KURT REHER,
    FREDERICK SEYKORA & ELEANOR SLATKIN: cello
BUDDY CHILDERS, CLYDE REASINGER, JACK SHELDON & ANTHONY TERRAN: trumpet
MILT BERNHARDT, RICHARD LEITH, LEW McCREARY, GEORGE ROBERTS & FRANK
    ROSOLINO: trombone
JOHN CAVE, VINCENT DeROSA, DAVID DUKE, ARTHUR MAEBE & RICHARD PERISSI:
    french horn
JOHN LOWE: sax
SHORTY ROGERS: arrangement

recorded 10/31/67 - 2/15/68

Davy was the one cast member who had the least pre-Monkees experience as a musician and was the most content to let Don Kirshner and the Powers-That-Be do whatever they wanted with the music. So it is somewhat surprising that Davy actually produced more material than any of the Monkees other than Mike. He was initially hired as an actor to play the part of a rock star and he was the most secure in not actually being a recording artist or a musician himself. The question then becomes, why did Davy go on to produce so much more recorded material than Micky or Peter? Sure, he wasn't the experimenter that Micky was or the perfectionist that Peter was, so he was able to get his stuff recorded and done a lot faster than either of them. But what was his motivation to bother producing or writing songs at all when there were already professionals hired to do this part of the job for him?

I think a large part of the reason can be gleaned from gripes Davy made about Mike shoehorning songs like "Tapioca Tundra" onto the b-sides of singles in order to get more money from royalties. Davy clearly saw that there was cash to be made on the Monkees' music and wanted to hop onto that gravy train. He was not writing and producing songs to try and express himself, which may be why almost all of them are co-written with someone else who had a little more musical knowledge, or perhaps talent, than Davy did on his own.

As for his own personal taste it is hard to say whether or not this kind of music is what he liked to listen to, but Davy knew that the most commercial thing he could do as a teen idol was to push the sappy romantic angle. In some ways, Davy was a throwback to those dark days between Elvis and the Beatles when bland mannequins such as Frankie Avalon and Fabian ruled the rock'n'roll charts. If you listen to Davy's pre-Monkees solo album, other than the cover of the Bob Dylan tune, it sounds like it could've been recorded in some sort of Beatles-less alternate universe.

When asked at the time to describe his style Davy would often reply that it was "Broadway Rock." This is a combination that may have seemed ludicrous at the time and hasn't really flourished since. About the only artist to really do this kind of music after Davy was Tom Jones. Since Tom wasn't around at the time, the artist that Davy was mostly modeling himself after at this point is the now forgotten British singer, Andrew Newely. Andrew is now best known for being a big inspiration for another David Jones, the one who had to change his name to David Bowie to keep from being confused with the Monkee.

"The Girl I Left Behind Me" may have one of the most convoluted histories in the entire history of the Monkees. The song was written by Neil Sedaka and Carole Bayer and the first version was produced by them in November of 1966 for possible inclusion on the second album. That version of the song may or may not have ever actually gotten finished, but either way the Don Kirshner passed on the song for *More Of The Monkees*. Nearly a year later, Davy's first attempt at producing post-Chip Douglas was a medley of this song and "A Girl Named Love." The second half of this song never got vocals recorded and was left unfinished. Davy then tried a second time to record "The Girl I Left Behind Me" alongside a bunch of other songs in February of 1968. This version was submitted for the album *The Birds, The Bees, & The Monkees*. Again the song got passed over. However by 1969, Lester Sill was looking for material for the *Instant Replay* album and either the first version produced by Neil Sedaka or the last version produced by Davy was used on that album. Unfortunately, there has been conflicting reports on to which version is which. They are both fairly similar and the song is so mushy and unremarkable, it is easy to understand how things got so mixed up. I'm still not quite sure what version of "The Girl I Left Behind Me" I currently have slotted in where; and frankly, I don't care enough about this tune to really listen and see if I can figure which one goes where.

Luckily, the medley version of the song is identifiable by the fact that it has a protracted ending that is supposed to be a second song Davy co-wrote with Charlie Smalls, who later wrote the musical *The Wiz*. You can hear a bit of the two of them singing the song in an episode of the TV series, but you don't really get much of a feel for what the missing lyrics are like. After "Hard To Believe" Davy was still casting around for songwriters willing to share credit and craft material that Davy felt was appropriate for him. "A Girl Named Love" is the only tangible result we have of the Davy Jones/Charlie Smalls songwriting partnership. It certainly sounds like there could've been some good interesting work from these two, but the one piece we have is too fragmentary to really tell. It certainly would've been better than the material he came up with in conjunction with Steve Pitts.

Next Davy tried writing with Don DeMieri and Robert Dick for the sappy **"Ceiling In My Room"**. This seems to be an attempt to write a teen idol version of Frank Sinatra's "My Way". However it is very difficult to stir up any sympathy for the lonely life of a millionaire singer with hundreds of adoring fans. Or maybe the singer is just deluding himself that he is a superstar while lying on his back staring at the ceiling. The lyrics are a little confusing; and even Davy's double-tracked vocals can't seem to decide if it's a "yes" or a "no" before the title refrain. Either way, Davy comes off as super-whiny here in the lyrics. At least the music, which is a little more stripped down and free of extraneous orchestration than most Davy's productions at this time, comes out okay. It's still a super-syrupy slow ballad, but it has a nice lounge-y feel to it. Davy would certainly do worse than this.

The normally objective Andrew Sandoval does let a bit of judgment slip out in his book, The Monkees: The Day-By-Day Story of the 60s TV Pop Sensation. In the entry for February 6th, 1968 he refers to the day's work as "the most productive albeit bland session of the year." The first song recorded on this day was a remake of **"War Games"**. I'm not sure what Davy's objections to Mike's production of "War Games" were, but the version he come up with here is thoroughly more pretentious and silly. The guitar does still seem to be doing something vaguely country, but it is overwhelmed by the marching snare, strings, and horns. While I do applaud the sentiment of the lyrics, they really aren't much deeper than saying "war is bad." Davy and co-writer Steve Pitts seem to be trying to say something sarcastic in the way it is portrayed as a harmless sports event on

TV, but we never really sure if the audience is culpable in these "games" or who's orchestrating all of this for the otherwise passive listener. While the reality of the Vietnam War was something that needed to be addressed at the time, Davy was smart enough to realize that there was no way the Powers-That-Be were going to let him release anything that directly addressed the situation; so perhaps the extended silly metaphor was necessary.

The shellacked on layers of horns and strings continues with another Jones/Pitts original, **"Dream World"**. This song at least has a subject matter that Davy was more at home with: the love of a girl. The lyrics seem to exhorting the girl in question to give up her fantasies of finding a better man than Davy and just settling down with him. That is kind of an unsettling message. Of course, Davy doesn't want to make himself out to be the kind of guy that someone settles for, so the crux of the song is that the girl's delusions are not just unrealistic, but somehow psychologically disturbed. The song is a little more up-tempo than "War Games" which helps a lot, but it is still sickly sweet. This is the kind of stuff that young girls would eat up with a spoon and Lester Sills used it to be the leadoff track on the album *The Birds, The Bees, & The Monkees*.

While almost everything Davy produced for himself tended to be mawkish and maudlin, he could rock out if he wanted to. Case in point: **"Changes"**, this song was written by Davy Jones and Steve Pitts with the intention of being the title track for the movie. However, "Changes" wound up being just the working title for the film, which was eventually re-titled "Untitled" before being called *Head*. To complicate matters, the Monkees' 1970 album was also entitled *Changes*, but "Changes" song wasn't released on that album either. This song definitely feels like a sibling to Goffin & King's "Look Down" and holds its own next to that one very nicely. The repeated vibra-slap is a nice touch. The lyrics are faux-profound, but don't get in the way of enjoying the song. Shorty Roger's horn arrangement is great. It's a shame that Davy didn't trust himself to do more material like this instead of relying on his usual trite love-songs.

Not only did Davy re-do Carole Sayer's "The Girl I Left Behind Me" but he also completed a version of her **"We Were Made For Each Other"**. The song was first attempted by Chip Douglas on his own after the rest of the Monkees stopped playing with him, but was left unfinished as none of the Monkees would sing on it. Chip's version prominent banjo and has a nice lilting folk-rock feel to it. Davy's version is pretty much par for the course. I am beginning to run out of synonyms for dreck. The song features some prominent harpsichord which shows up on a couple of Davy's productions of this time period. The melody is a little high for Davy's naturally baritone voice. The key change at 1:38 vainly tries to add some excitement to a song that is already starting to bore. There is not much worth remarking on here. The best thing you can say about it is that it is short.

The last song recorded on February 6th 1968 is **"It's Nice To Be With You"**. Again this is very middle-of-the-road. While the song is clearly marketed for the teen market, it is something of a precursor to the genre of Adult Contemporary. Davy's voice is not a good fit for this wannabe-Sinatra stuff. Pretty much everything I said about "We Were Made For Each Other" can also be applied here. The song was written by Jerry Goldstein, best known for co-writing "I Want Candy" and "My Boyfriend's Back" as well as producing and writing for the band War with Eric Burdon. Because of this pedigree it is a little more polished than Davy Jones and Steve Pitts would've come up with, but it is still far from good or even interesting. In fact it may be too polished and a more naive songwriter, such as Davy Jones, may have inadvertently come up with something more notable.

Davy did co-write all three songs that he produced when he went into the studio a week later, but unfortunately none of them have that amateur charm. I am guessing in part due to the influence of co-writer Steve Pitts. It's hard to talk about the first song, **"The Poster"** without mentioning the Beatles' "Being For The Benefit Of Mr. Kite." Clearly the *Sgt. Pepper* track was the inspiration for this song, while both were sparked by a vintage circus poster. The Beatles' song is a dark and surreal nightmare of strange images. Davy's song is a chirpy light tune with absolutely no weight or meaning to the lyrics whatsoever other than "the circus is coming to town!" The comparisons are hard to avoid, and it does the Monkees' song no favors. This song was also included on *The Birds, The Bees, & The Monkees* which Lester Sill seems to have arranged to showcase Mike at his trippiest and Davy at his drippiest.

Both **"I'm Gonna Try"** and **"The Party"** sound like they have the same backing track with just different melodies and lyrics recorded on top of them. I even went so far as to play both at the same time to see if this was actually true. It isn't technically but you can get pretty far into listening to both simultaneously before it runs into the unlistenable cacophony that most songs create when played in tandem. The tempo is identical. The opening chords on the strings are exactly the same. "The Party" may have the edge in that it has a bit of a change in the slowing ascending chords that build under the line "I think that I might just fall for you." The lyrics of "I'm Gonna Try" are a little more unexpected, being a self-confidence booster rather than the usual "I found a girl." For all the joking about these songs being indistinguishable, this pair presents the most damning evidence that it is true. While he may have had no interest in producing some sort of artistic masterpiece, Davy was going have to do something else if he was going to produce anything of any depth or lasting value as a producer.

DAVY JONES 2

1.) Smile 2:20
(written by Davy Jones)
first released as a bonus track on *Instant Replay*
May 10th, 1968

2.) You And I 2:14
(written by Davy Jones and Bill Chadwick)
from *Instant Replay*
May 10th, 1968

3.) Penny Music 2:40
(written by Michael Leonard, Bobby Weinstein, and Jon Stroll)
first released on *Missing Links Vol. III*
May 1st, 1969

4.) Opening Night 3:45
(written by Charlie Smalls)
first released as a bonus track on *The Monkees Present*
May 1st, 1969

5.) French Song 2:26 *
(written by Bill Chadwick)
from *The Monkees Present*
June 27th, 1969

6.) How Can I Tell You? 3:13
(written by Davy Jones and Bill Chadwick)
first released as a bonus track on *The Monkees Present*
June 27th, 1969

7.) If I Knew 2:23 *
(written by Davy Jones and Bill Chadwick)
from *The Monkees Present*
July 1st, 1969

8.) The Good Earth
(written by Ben Nisbet)
first released as a bonus track on *The Monkees Present*
July 21st, 1969

9.) If You Have The Time 2:09 *
(written by Davy Jones and Bill Chadwick)
first released on *Missing Links Vol. I*
August 6th, 1969

10.) Time And Time Again 2:50 *
(written by Davy Jones and Bill Chadwick)
first released on *Missing Links Vol. III*
August 6th, 1969

UNFINISHED SONGS FROM THESE SESSIONS:
That's What I Like Loving You (written by Davy Jones and Steve Pitts)

Produced by Davy Jones
* Produced by Davy Jones & Bill Chadwick

MUSICIANS:
LOUIE SHELTON, FRANK BUGBEE, & DAVID COHEN: guitar
MAX BENNETT & JOE OSBORN: bass
HAL BLAINE & JOHN GUERIN: drums
MICHAEL RUBINI: piano, organ, calliope
EMIL RICHARDS: percussion
PAUL BEAVER: moog synthesizer
BILL CHADWICK, GERRY McGEE, LOUIE SHELTON, & NEIL YOUNG: guitar (on "Smile"
    and "You And I")
LARRY KNETCHEL: organ and electric piano (on "Smile" and "You And I")
DAVY JONES & BILL CHADWICK: backing vocals

recorded 5/10/68 and 5/1/69 - 8/6/69

While I may have been a little harsh on Davy's last playlist, this one is much better. First off Davy has swapped co-writer Steve Pitts for Bill Chadwick who also wrote "Zor And Zam", "Of You", and "Talking To The Wall" from Mike's solo album *Tantamount To Treason Vol. 1*. Also, Davy is trying really hard for a more mature and sophisticated sound. Perhaps he was worried about being pegged as teeny-bopper while his demographic inevitably began to get older This is not exactly Sinatra, but it still whittles down some of the bombast from the last playlist substantially. Of course, another reason for this more stripped down approach may have been as much a financial decision as it was an artistic one. With the Monkees' rapidly declining record sales, Colgems was a lot less interested in ponying up the dough for all the strings and horns that were lavishly slathered all over Davy's previous set of sessions.

Whatever the reason, Davy does seem a little more invested in trying to make a good music and less interested in simply giving the audience what he thinks they want. While Davy may not have suddenly discovered a misunderstood artist under the layers of artifice, this cool jazz vibe suits him much better, and is infinitely easier to listen to, than the Vegas-y "Broadway Rock" that he had been peddling previously. The sound on these tracks is all piano and vibes and flute and moog synthesizer; all of which can bring to mind elevator Muzak, but can also be used judiciously. This is definitely an improvement on the over-the-top schlock Davy was producing. If he continued to improve at the rate, who knows where Davy might have ended up as a musical artist. However, once the Monkees ended Davy seemed to show no more interest in growing as a musician or producer. For his solo career, Davy was happy to let the professionals deal with the actual music while he just came in and sang what they told him to. Just listen to Davy's first post-Monkees album, *Davy Jones* if you don't believe me.

Before he began work with Bill Chadwick on the bulk of this playlist in May of 1969, nearly a year prior Davy produced a pair of tunes on his own. These two songs offer an interesting look at the transition between the two different sets of sessions. The first song recorded **"Smile"** is the only solo Davy Jones composition credit in the entire Monkees' catalog. It's a fairly standard Broadway-type number with the usual, "the show must go on" type of lyrics that Davy was often fond of. Still there's nothing wrong with it and if Davy really wanted to concentrate on songwriting (and keep from having to share his royalties with various co-writers) he could've done it.

One of the more interesting things about these two songs is the inclusion of Neil Young on guitar. Neil also played on Goffin & King's session for "As We Go Along." I'm not quite sure what Neil was thinking at the time. Perhaps he was uncertain of his ability to maintain a solo career post-Buffalo Springfield and seriously thought that he could work as an anonymous session musician in L.A. Or maybe he just wanted to piss-off bandmate Stephen Still by having a Monkee-friend of his own. Whatever the reason, Neil's work on "Smile" and "As We Go Around" is just basic strumming that anyone could've done. The other song that Davy taped that session is a different matter altogether and features some very distinctive lead guitar soloing from Neil.

This song is simply entitled **"You And I"** and it is easily the best thing that Davy ever produced. The criticism with Davy is that he was not as personally involved in his songs in the same way that Mike or Peter were. "You And I" is not this way at all. It is plainly obvious that Davy really feels what he's singing about. Granted, what he's singing about is how pissed he is that his audience seems to have moved on to the next big thing and left him behind, but he genuinely is angry about it. Neil Young's proto-grunge guitar playing make sense within the context of this song. It is a truly furious, frustrated number, and Davy would never get close to being as personally connected to again. In fact, he didn't even try to produce anything for nearly a year afterwards. These two songs almost make a really short playlist (or single) by themselves; and even though they were recorded closer to the last sessions than this one, the improvement in these tunes makes them feel like more of a fit with this chapter.

Even Davy must've sensed how effective "You And I" was and enlisted its co-writer, Bill Chadwick, to work with him on almost of the next batch of songs. But first Davy would record another pair of tunes, which even though he did have anything to do with the writing of either, were both lyrically focused on the life and struggles of being a good old-fashioned entertainer. If you take these two tracks along with "Ceiling In My Room" and "Smile" you would almost have a "concept EP" of songs about backstage drama, wannabe actors, flashbulbs and greasepaint.

"Penny Music" almost sounds like it could've come from the musical *Oliver!* It's a charming tale about street musician. During the verses Davy comments on this older and unpolished violinist with something somewhere between annoyance and bemusement. In the choruses, the POV switches to that of the struggling maestro. Despite many digs at the musician's abilities, the lyrics seem to be celebrating the old man's perseverance in the face of this lack of talent. The music itself does feature some marching snare, but is free of any actual violin. It's pretty tame, but certainly much better than most of the drivel from the first Davy Jones playlist.

While Davy sings in primarily in the third person about the entertainer in "Penny Music," he is the star of **"Opening Night"**. Again there are no strings and the horns are scaled back immensely, which is a good thing. The song is very jazz-cum-Broadway, which is not surprising because it was written by Davy's former co-writer, Charlie Smalls, who also wrote *The Wiz*. Of course, the protagonist of the lyrics here is not a desperate but talentless musician, but rather an actor who is nervous about his performance because he only wants to put on as good of a show as possible. By the end, although it is not stated, it seems that Davy has put on his big show and it was a well-received success. The extended sax solo at the end does go on a bit longer than it needs to before fading out. This is nowhere as good as "You And I," but at least it's less chintzy than "Penny Music." This track bodes well for the rest of the playlist.

"French Song" is not French. The lyrics are not in French. In fact, the setting of song is never overtly stated, although one could reasonably assume that it takes place in Paris. There is no reason to call this "French Song" other than the mood the song establishes feels like a French film and the instrumentation and arrangement is somewhat similar to French popular music. Unlike Mike who willfully mistitles his songs, Davy has no such perverse streak. But since the song has no repeating lyrical hook he had to call it something, so "French Song" it is. Although it is possible that Bill Chadwick wrote this song by himself. Bill has occasionally insinuated that Davy's co-writing credit on some of these songs was not earned, but rather granted after the fact, as an incentive for him to record this material.

Still this is one of the best songs Davy ever produced. It has a very cool jazz, late night feel. The vibes, organ, and flute are a lovely combination and the restraint Davy applies not only to the arrangement but also his vocals is so much better than the layers of orchestration he was often wont to do. Davy, who as a Broadway actor is used to singing to the rafters, does a great job of pulling back here. While Davy may never have the critical caché of Michael Nesmith, had he done more material in this vein he certainly wouldn't have been as easy to dismiss him as an artist.

The stripped down arrangement for **"How Can I Tell You?"** sounds pretty full and fits the song really well with just brushed drums, piano, acoustic guitar, and upright bass. There does seem to be a bit of a blank space in the song two minutes in, where one would assume that some sort of solo would have gone. The song isn't as cool as "French Song" and some of the other productions at this time, but it is certain that Davy was trying a little harder to make something more substantial with his music. Maybe he just felt he was getting old and looked a little silly always singing to a bunch of teen and pre-teen girls.

"If I Knew" is another song in the same mold as "French Song" and "How Can I Tell You?" The song has some lovely harmony and backing vocal parts overdubbed by Davy, but it is a still a very small combo playing here. The lyrics are focused on romantic entanglements and how much love he feels for the subject of the song. Still, the sigh that Davy lets out at the end of the tune doesn't sound as calculated or forced as most of the material foisted on Davy during the early years of the Monkees.

While this more mature version of Davy is certainly a welcome improvement; even a sophisticated Davy couldn't do a decent version of "The Day We Fall In Love." **"The Good Earth"** is also a spoken word poem; and while this track doesn't have the schmaltzy musical backing (or any musical backing), it is still pretty dreadful. This time the love in question is far more universal and the words aim for some sort of deep thoughts on the nature of man. However it still comes off as pretentious and annoying. There is really no need to listen to this one more than once.

Davy's last two productions are a bit more up-tempo. Both feature prominent use of the new synthesizer technology as well having the word "time" in the title. **"If You Have The Time"** is another jaunty music hall type song that really should be left to Harry Nilsson. The simplified instrumentation is nice. The primitive synth solo is pretty cool for its time and still holds up pretty well now. In place of Davy's usual strings and horns are just lots of wordless backing vocals. Even Davy must've realized how slight the song is as it clocks in at just over two minutes.

"Time And Time Again" sounds like an attempt to split the difference between the more chipper numbers like "If You Have The Time" and the cool jazz feel of songs like "French Song." There's another early synthesizer solo that is not nearly as audacious as the one on "If You Have The Time," but acquits itself ably enough. Again, there are layers of backing vocals compensating for the smaller size of the band. This song was briefly considered for inclusion on the album *Changes* and would've been a fine addition to that album. At this point Davy seems to have actively become interested in growing as a producer and could have, if he wanted to, really stretched himself musically in his imminent solo career. He certainly had a head start with the most popularity and clout at the time of the Monkees disbanding, but decided against seriously pursuing that path post-Monkees. Perhaps because it was too much hard work and he wasn't all that interested. Or perhaps he knew that no matter how great his artistic success in this area, he would never recapture the triumph of his earlier success and decided not to bother.

PETER TORK

1.) Lady's Baby 2:30
(written by Peter Tork)
first released on *Missing Links Vol. I*
November 16th, 1967

2.) (I Prithee) Do Not Ask For Love 3:48
(written by Michael Martin Murphey)
first released as a bonus track on *"The Birds, The Bees, & The Monkees"*
December 3rd, 1967

3.) Seeger's Theme 0:45
(written by Pete Seeger)
first released on *Missing Links Vol. II*
January 14th, 1968

4.) Alvin 0:27
(written by Nicholas Thorkelson)
first released as a bonus track on *"The Birds, The Bees, & The Monkees"*
January 20th, 1968

5.) Merry Go Round 1:44
(written by Peter Tork and Diane Hildebrand)
first released on *Missing Links Vol. III*
January 22nd, 1968

6.) Long Title: Do I Have to Do This All Over Again? 2:36
(written by Peter Tork)
from the soundtrack to *Head*
January 25th, 1968

7.) Can You Dig It? 3:28
(written by Peter Tork)
from the soundtrack to *Head*
January 28th, 1968

8.) Tear The Top Right Off My Head 2:06
(written by Peter Tork)
first released on *Missing Links Vol. III*
February 5th, 1968

9.) Come On In 3:11
(written by Jo Mapes)
first released on *Missing Links Vol. II*
February 8th, 1968

UNFINISHED SONGS FROM THESE SESSIONS:
Who Will Buy? (written by Lionel Bart)
Lance's (written by Lance Wakely)

Produced by Peter Tork

MUSICIANS:
PETER TORK: guitar, bass, banjo, tack piano
LANCE WAKELY: guitar, bass, harmonica
STEPHEN STILLS: guitar
DEWEY MARTIN & BUDDY MILES: drums
DAVY JONES, PETER TORK, & KAREN HARVEY HAMMER: background vocals

recorded 11/16/67 - 2/8/68

Peter was never destined, nor particularly desirous, of solo stardom. Pete was always the opposite of prolific when it came to songwriting. As a lead vocalist, Pete was an acquired taste, to say the least. Where Peter really flourished was as a member of a band, like he was during the Chip Douglas days. This is where Peter's prowess on a number of different instruments in several genres was truly an asset. His graciousness in letting others have the spotlight allowed him to do the heavy-lifting in the background while the other three got to really shine. This modesty, bordering on pathological shyness, did allow Pete to play the dummy on the TV show with such charm and no apparent bitterness.

This lack of guile and ego did make it hard for Peter to stand up and assert himself. Despite all the time and effort he put into several of his songs, almost none of them were released during the Monkees' original run. Two of the only three Tork compositions that did get released were both on the *Head* soundtrack. Lester Sill even omitted such quick inoffensive fare as "Alvin" leaving the released version of *The Birds, The Bees, & The Monkees* surprisingly lopsided and Tork-free.

It's no surprise that when Don Kirshner was ousted and the boys were put in charge that Pete did not feel the need to take any solo lead vocals, but was content to share both "Shades Of Gray" and the re-make of

"Words." It's also unsurprising, but disappointing, that Peter Tork's first solo project after the Monkees, Release, never managed to release anything. I truly hope that there's at least something recorded by Release sitting somewhere in the vaults - perhaps even the title tune Peter wrote for Bob Rafelson and Bert Schneider next film *Easy Rider*, a tune which they then rejected.

When the band concept fell apart and each cast member went to record on their own, Peter's interest began to wane and he soon left the Monkees project altogether. If one wanted to expand out this playlist to album-length you could use some of the instrumental cuts that ended up on the *Headquarters Sessions* box set. Unfinished tracks such as Bach's "Two Part Invention in F" and the traditional "Cripple Creek" are both worthy additions to any hypothetical 60s Peter Tork solo LP.

What we are left with is a sadly small pool of material that Pete actually produced for himself. He did not seem to have any interest in producing a whole Monkees album like Mike always wanted to do. While he did have Micky sing lead on two of his songs, "Can You Dig It?" and "Tear The Top Right Off My Head," Peter also laid down his own lead vocals for both. He also apparently recorded an as-of-yet unreleased version of "Who Will Buy?" from the musical *Oliver!* presumably for Davy to sing. Who knows what that pairing would've sounded like. Not only did Peter record very little material, but most of the songs he recorded are pretty short. "Alvin" and "Seeger's Theme" are both under a minute and "Merry-Go-Round" isn't even two minutes long.

While there may not have been a lot of different titles in the Peter Tork oeuvre, there are a lot of different versions of each tune. Either because he was a perfectionist or just because he liked recording and had nothing else to record, there are four or five distinct versions of "Lady's Baby", three or four "Seeger's Theme"s and at least a couple of "Merry-Go-Round"s. You can certainly pad out this playlist by including multiple versions of each song, but for the most part each subsequent revision of the song doesn't add anything substantial to the last.

Looking at Peter Tork's small selection of material, what was his vision for the Monkees? Despite his oft-professed love of Bach and Pete Seeger, there is not a lot of harpsichord or banjo on these tracks. Instead Peter seems to be trying to sound like Buffalo Springfield. Not only does Peter look like Stephen Stills, but frequently employed Stills and Springfield drummer Dewey Martin for his sessions. Another big hallmark of Peter's sessions is a tendency to have the drummer either break into double or half time during various sections giving the impression of multiple tempos going within each song.

The song that Peter spent the most time on, and seemed to have the most trouble with, is the infamous **"Lady's Baby"**. There's some recordings that are more acoustic and others that are more electric. There's mixes with the sounds of an infant included and others without. Some have drums and some don't. But none of these versions are terribly different from each other.

It's a pretty song with a fragile melody that Peter's voice isn't quite up for, but still it's obviously a sincere and heartfelt sentiment. The lyrics are all about how his girlfriend's young son makes him love her more and want to try and be a more of a grown-up. The song jumps into double time when he sings about "running" or "chasing" but quickly drops back into its laid back groove. As good of a song as it was, and as hard as Peter worked on it, it's not surprising that Lester Sill passed over on this track. This kind of maturity is very different from the character that Peter played on the TV show.

While Peter got to do an Indian arrangement of **"(I Prithee) Do Not Ask For Love"** on the TV special, cementing his position as the George Harrison of the Monkees, his studio production of this song is made entirely of electric guitars. While Mike brought this song to the group via his friend Michael Martin Murphey, Peter seems to have really wanted to sing it. The arrangement here is very stark and off-putting, with chords slashing on the beat constantly with no rhythmic variation. It would be an interesting effect if there were some drums or something maintaining a real groove for this play off of, but as it stands now it really seems like more of a demo that a fully realized song. This is too bad because "(I Prithee) Do Not Ask For Love" is a tune that fits Peter's voice very nicely.

Another song with a demo version, an acoustic version, an electric version, and an alternate version all currently in circulation, **"Seeger's Theme"** is merely a brief instrumental. Pete Seeger wrote this fragment under the equally grandiose, but less egotistical, title of "Theme From The Goofing Off Suite." While the different takes do have some difference, it probably didn't need to be recorded this many times as it is under a minute long. While it is an impressive showcase for Peter's abilities on a number of instruments, there's not much to say about the tune. It almost would've made more sense as incidental music on the TV show that released on an album. Tork probably just wanted to get his idol, Pete Seeger, some songwriting royalties as well try to turn a few Monkees fans on to his music.

He probably also wanted to spread the wealth with his brother, Nick, which is why Peter recorded the even shorter a Capella tune, **"Alvin"**. This would've been perfect to fill the "Peter Percival Patterson..." slot on *The Birds, The Bees, & The Monkees*. Its omission may be some sort of vendetta against Peter on behalf of Lester Sill. More likely, Lester knew the album would sell the same whether or not he a short Peret Tork a capella track, and decided that he didn't want to have to pay the royalties of another songwriter. It's too bad because this is a fun little tune about flushing a pet baby alligator. Unlike a lot of stuff that Peter was recording at the time, this would've been a good fit for his TV persona.

Slightly longer than the previous two tracks, but still not quite full song length, is **"Merry Go Round"**. Peter collaborated on with "Your Auntie Grizelda" co-writer, Diane Hildebrand. However, this song is not nearly as contrived for Pete's on-screen character. Rather this is a "very serious" piece that feels sort of like Joni Mitchell's "Big Yellow Taxi" or "Circle Game" but not as good. Despite being under two minutes, the tempo is so slow that the song seems to take forever. Again, there are a couple of versions of this song. The demo version might be the best iteration. The production is very similar to Peter's version of "(I Prithee) Do No Ask For Love" with piano and/or organ replacing the slashing chords on the guitar but lacking any sort of rhythmic bed to tie the whole thing together. Given the low register in which Peter sings it, one might almost suspect that the tape was meant to be sped up before the track was released. This would've made a short song even shorter, but this is pure speculation on my part. Other than "Lady's Baby," Peter has not yet shown any interest in producing a full-length song for himself.

Luckily, **"Long Title: Do I Have To Do This All Over Again?"** is a real song. While one might not expect that Peter could really rock, he really does a good job on this song. Unlike many other Peter tracks, he seems to have a really clear vision on this one and we are not inundated with a plethora of alternate versions. Other than "Your Auntie Grizelda" this is the only full lead vocal Pete got during the Monkees original run, being part of the soundtrack to *Head* and featured in the dance party scene. The song features a pretty cool shift to waltz time during the instrumental break that is nice change of pace without feeling grafted on. As much time and effort that Peter expended on "Lady's Baby," "Long Title" is a much better track and evidences a self-confidence that is sorely missing from many of Peter's songs.

That lack of confidence may be why Peter let Micky sing his song **"Can You Dig It?"** Listening to Peter's guide vocals on outtake version of this song, it's hard not to that think he made the right choice. But honestly, I prefer Peter's weak, watery singing on here, but I can see why most people do not. This is song cribs the faux-raga sound that George Harrison was employing with the Beatles at the time; although the scales and arrangements here are far more Arabian than Indian. This song was first demo'd during *Headquarters* as an instrumental entitled "Tentatively." The lyrics are supposedly deep hippy stuff that really doesn't mean that much. The musicians pull off a very non-Western sound without resorting to actually using sitars or tablas. While this is not as driving as "Long Title," it is pretty funky with some especially nimble bass playing by Peter.

Peter also lets Micky try singing **"Tear The Top Right Off My**

Head", which is odd since the song works so nicely with Peter's on-screen goofball character. Micky does okay singing it, but this song is far more in Pete's limited vocal wheelhouse. The song ping-pongs back and forth between light folksy acoustic verses and heavy electric choruses. The guitar solo is even split between both halves of the record, and Peter lets out an overly overdubbed "Take it, Lance!" that brings to mind Mike's "pick it, Luther" from "Papa Gene's Blues". The whole thing is great silly fun and a shame it wasn't released sometime during the Monkees' original run, although you can hear Micky and Peter do a brief acoustic snippet during the episode "Hitting The High Seas."

The last song Peter produced for the Monkees is, oddly enough, an invitation to **"Come On In"**. The original by Jo Mapes is something a fairly straight-forward folk tune that was also covered by the Association in a very standard folk-rock arrangement of the time. Peter turns this into his most Buffalo Springfield-like production. The song even goes into double time at certain points, as was often the case in Peter's songs. This is probably the closest to an average Peter Tork track as he has ever recorded. It's very nice and well-done but there's not much to say about it. It's a shame Peter wasn't able to get more stuff recorded before giving up on The Monkees. With songs as good as this are his baseline, he may have even given Nesmith a run for his money, in terms of quality if not quantity.

MICKY DOLENZ

1.) Zor And Zam 2:13
(written by Bill Chadwick and John Chadwick)
from *The Birds, The Bees, & The Monkees*
January 7th, 1968

2.) Shorty Blackwell 5:43
(written by Micky Dolenz)
from *Instant Replay*
January 19th, 1968

3.) D. W. Washburn 2:51 *
(written by Jerry Leiber and Mike Stoller)
released as a single
February 17th, 1968

4.) Rosemarie 2:29
(written by Micky Dolenz)
first released on *Missing Links Vol. I*
February 19th, 1968

5.) Don't Say Nothin' Bad (About My Baby) 2:08
(written by Gerry Goffin and Carole King)
first released on as a bonus track on *The Birds, The Bees, & The Monkees*
February 24th, 1968

6.) Shake 'Em Up And Let 'Em Roll 2:11
(written by Jerry Leiber and Mike Stoller)
first released on *Missing Links Vol. III*
February 24th, 1968

7.) Just A Game 1:50
(written by Micky Dolenz)
from *Instant Replay*
April 9th, 1968

8.) Mommy And Daddy 2:08
(written by Micky Dolenz)
from *The Monkees Present*
August 1st, 1968

9.) We'll Be Back In A Minute 0:22
(written by Micky Dolenz)
first released on *Missing Links Vol. III*
July 1st, 1969

10.) Bye Bye Baby Bye Bye 2:21
(written by Micky Dolenz and Ric Klein)
from *The Monkees Present*
July 16th, 1969

11.) Midnight Train 2:03
(written by Micky Dolenz)
from *Changes*
July 16th, 1969

12.) Little Girl 2:01
(written by Micky Dolenz)
from *The Monkees Present*
August 14th, 1969

13.) Pillow Time 2:32
(written by Janelle Scott and Matt Willis)
from *The Monkees Present*
August 14th, 1969

Produced by Micky Dolenz, except
* Produced by Micky Dolenz and Lester Sill

MUSICIANS:
LOUIE SHELTON, TOMMY TEDESCO & KEITH ALLISON: guitar
MAX BENNETT, JOE OSBORN, RAY POHLMAN, & CHIP
    DOUGLAS: bass
JIM GORDON, HAL BLAINE, & EARL PALMER: drums
MICHAEL RUBINI: piano, harpsichord
MICKY DOLENZ: acoustic guitar, piano, drums
HENRY DILTZ: banjo, clarinet
JAMES BURTON: banjo
TOMMY MORGAN: harmonica
PETER TORK: acoustic guitar (on "Rosemarie")
EDDIE HOH: drums (on "Shake 'Em Up)
GEORGE BERRES, ANATOL KAMINSKY, BERNARD KUNDELL, ERNO NEUFELD,
    NATHAN ROSS, & JOSEPH STEPANSKY: violin
JUSTIN DiTULLIO, ARMAND KAPROFF, & EDGAR LUSTGARTEN: cello
BUD BRISBOIS, BUDDY CHILDERS, CARROLL LEWIS, OLIVER MITCHELL, RAY
    TRISCARI, & STU WILLIAMSON: trumpet

GEORGE ROBERTS, KENNY SHROYER, LOU BLACKBURN, HERBIE HARPER, & LEW
   McCREARY: trombone
VINCENT DeROSA, DAVID DUKE, & DICK PERISSI: french horn
BILL HOOD: sax
JOHN KITZMILLER: tuba
DON McGINNIS: brass
RONNIE LANG, TED NASH, & BUD SHANK: flute
JOE PORCARO & LARRY BUNKER: percussion

recorded 1/7/68 - 8/14/69

Conventional wisdom has it that when Bob & Bert hired the four guys
to play the Monkees they ended up with two musicians (Peter and Mike)
and two actors (Davy and Micky). While the truth is not quite as simple as
that, there is something to it. Micky was a child actor, best known for
starring in *Circus Boy* as a kid. While he did play some guitar and sang in a
band called The Missing Links prior to the Monkees, he certainly had never
played drums before being cast as the drummer. Micky was more
interested in acting than singing, and had auditioned for a number of shows
during the pilot season when he was cast in "The Monkees." While Micky
did have a wonderful innate ability as a singer, he was never really driven to
be an instrumentalist like Peter and a musical artist like Michael.

While Peter has often chided Micky for not going back into heavy
psychedelia after scoring big with the composition "Randy Scouse Git."
Anyone who was listened to Micky's post-*Headquarters* work knows that this
is not true. Certainly not anyone who has listened to "Shorty Blackwell."
While not a musical novice, what Micky did bring was a continuously
curious and inventive mind. Listening to Micky's work is even more of an
exciting discovery than even the overlooked Peter Tork. Sadly there is
almost as little of it, but because of the large number of lead vocals Dolenz
recorded it seems like there should be much more Micky-produced material
than there really is. Watching this amount of musical naïveté crossed with a
mad-scientist desire to experiment given unfettered studio access and an
extremely large potential audience is thoroughly fascinating.

"Zor And Zam" opens with a very similar snare drum pattern as "All
The King's Horses" and "Penny Music." The song was written by Bill
Chadwick with his brother John as the theme for unmade cartoon show
they were pitching. Some people have given this song credit for
popularizing the phrase "What is they gave a war and nobody came?"
While others say it originated with Bertolt Brecht. The truth is it stems
from the poem *The People, Yes* by Carl Sandburg and was used as the title of
a movie by Hy Averback in 1970. It was probably a Charlotte E. Keyes
article in McCall's magazine from 1966 rather than this obscure Monkees
track that brought the slogan to the attention of the hippie counter-culture
movement.

The song itself is pretty cool, with a faux-military sound that befits the words. The lyrics are a pretty obvious parable for the futility of war in general without going into any of the specifics of how to make that happen. Micky does a nice job of adding instruments and chords throughout the arrangement having the song slowly build through its entire running time. The mix featured on the last aired episode of the TV series, also directed by Micky, may be slightly better as it has fewer horns and a sparser production, but either way, it's a great song. This is not the last directly political song Micky attempts on this playlist.

While Peter spent a lot of studio time and money making different versions of "Lady's Baby," Micky spent nearly as long working on just one production of **"Shorty Blackwell"**. This is a production with a capital P. Nearly as long as "Writing Wrongs," but a lot more complicated, this song is like "Randy Scouse Git" taken to the nth degree. The song opens with a bombastic fanfare only to go quickly into a silly-voiced a Capella falsetto repetition of the title. That there is a perfect encapsulation of this song, with all sorts of bits and pieces coming and going, sometimes abruptly, sometimes overlapping.

The verses start out with just piano and drums, but then horns are added and the whole thing turns minor. There's repeated exhortations of "He's going mad!" before we settle back into the regular verse pattern. Then there's a weird tick-tock part before going into a solo piano part that transitions the whole song from 4/4 to 6/8. Coco and Micky's vocals in addition to the horns jump in on this before going into a very show-stopping rendition of a new verse. "I've been away" is repeated a couple of times before the whole song drops down to a jazzy 5/4 bit where Micky and Coco sing "I am I." While all this chaos may seem too random to be enjoyable there is a flow through all of this. Micky's sister Coco does most of the singing here. The lyrics are stray thoughts and other random observations about Micky's cat. This is way over-the-top, and a more experienced songwriter may have saved some of the sections from the song to develop into their own songs; but "Shorty Blackwell" really works mainly because it's fearless in its everything-and-the-kitchen-sink mentality.

"D.W. Washburn" on the other hand is relatively straight-forward. When Davy dons the straw hat and tries to do this type of material, it is meant as cutesy. When Micky does it, become full-blown vaudeville. He cranks up his best Jimmy Cagney impression for the vocals. The story is the odd tale of a homeless bum who rejects help because he sees his current life as much more pleasant and carefree than the constraints put upon him by the square world. I'm not sure why Micky has such affection for this anachronistic pastiche, but there a couple more tunes coming up that seem to be Micky's fallback position when he's not crafting grand experiments like "Shorty Blackwell."

"Rosemarie" another Dolenz penned original is not nearly as epic or audacious as "Shorty Blackwell." Still it is pretty darn strange. It's a horn driven-number of the type that the remaining three Monkees were doing during their 1969 tour with Sam & The Goodtimers. Micky seems far more certain of the music than the lyrics as there are a number of versions out there with him just mumbling or making up words. However, it sounds better once he's got his lyrics finalized, although the lyrics themselves don't mean much. It is a big production and a fun song to listen to. Some of the odder chord changes reflect Micky's relative inexperience as a songwriter, but they actually help make the song stand out from "Look Down", "Changes", or "You're So Good" which are all of a similar mold./

Both **"Don't Say Nothin' Bad (About My Baby)"** and **"Shake 'Em Up"** are cut from the same old-timey cloth as "D.W. Washburn." "Don't Say Nothin' Bad" was written by Goffin & King and 90% of the lyrics seem to be nothing but the title phrase repeated over and over again. It's as dumb as it gets, but harmless and luckily pretty short. Both "Shake 'Em Up" and "D.W. Washburn" were written by Leiber & Stoller and recorded around the same time by the Coasters. To add to the feel of this, "Shake 'Em Up" even features a clarinet solo by Henry Diltz, the Monkees' official photographer. Harry gets name-checked for his troubles. It feels like the success of "Winchester Cathedral" prompted Micky to indulge in these genre exercises. It's fun for a bit, but by this point the joke is getting a little old.

While "Shorty Blackwell" and "Rosemarie" are big productions, Micky's **"Just A Game"** seems in contrast to be as deliberately small as possible. The melody is not much sung as suggested. While there's a definite feeling of rejection from the lyrics, the vocal delivery treats them as a shrug. Despite all this nonchalance, the song does not come off as apathetic or half-hearted. A more experienced songwriter might've taken something like "Just A Game" and treated as a rough first draft for embellishing before finalizing the song. Micky instead makes a whole production out of what is only half a song. There's no bridge or chorus or other changes, just a series of verses coming one after another. It is very short song but still builds beautifully and then fades out resignedly. The instrumentation, especially the flute, almost has the same continental feel as Davy's "French Song." It certainly is a nice contrast or respite from the larger Micky Dolenz productions and makes the vaudeville-style songs seem that much more out-of-character.

Even more overtly political than "Zor And Zam" is **"Mommy And Daddy"**. At least with the original lyrics that Micky wrote. Lester Sill convinced him to tone down the words of this song for inclusion on *The Monkees Present*. Originally the lyrics did address the plight of the Native Americans, sex, and the death of JFK. Even neutered a bit, the furor is still there, just a little more subdued. While the music is more conventional than "Randy Scouse Git" or "Shorty Blackwell" the whole thing seethes. Micky even returned to playing the drums just for this one track. While the message of the lyrics is a bit confused, something along the lines of "don't trust anyone over 30", Dolenz sings them with a burning conviction. Micky's songwriting chops have certainly expanded as this song is catchy while not being as wooly or weird as past compositions. Certainly, the parts of the song aren't as jarringly put together. This is another great Micky track.

Another brief interlude into the vaudeville realm is **"We'll Be Back In A Minute"** sometimes also referred to as "Music Bridge." This is a really short burst of music to act as a bumper before the commercials during the re-runs of the TV show on Saturday mornings. It's not really meant to be listened to by itself, but I think would've worked really well at the end of side one of a vinyl record had it come out at the time. There's three different versions of it out there at least, but unlike Peter Tork, Micky isn't trying for a single definitive take as much as he's giving the TV producers a couple of options to choose from depending on the episode. It is a lot of fun with kazoos and goofy vocals. I'm not really excited about going back into "D.W. Washburn" territory, but at least this is very quick.

Micky continues to write more straightforward tunes with **"Bye Bye Baby Bye Bye"**. This song was co-written with his stand-in on the TV show, Ric Klein. "Bye Bye Baby Bye Bye" does have some banjo on it that almost threatens to take it to "Shake It Up" territory, but mostly it stays a furious acoustic rocker. The melody and lyrics take advantage of Micky remarkable speed and diction forcing him to spit out words like crazy. The sound, while primarily acoustic, is not folky. There is some great harmonica work on here. I love the way the backing vocals go "fa sol la" to build out a chord at one point. While not as remarkable as the more outré productions, this is a fun little number.

"Midnight Train" is much of the same acoustic mold, although it does tend to sound closer to a folk tune, especially with lyrics about locomotives. The harmonica is even more prominent and the drums are doing their best choo-choo impression. The demo version from the *Headquarters Sessions* makes this song seem like an *A Mighty Wind*-type folk number, but the production here is a little more Johnny Cash meets the New Vaudeville Band. The song, slowly builds up in tempo before ending with a chance for guitarist Louie Shelton to show off some really nice fast guitar runs. Micky does seem more confident in his ability to write and produce a song at this point. He is now less inclined to throw everything against the wall to see what sticks, which would be exhausting after a while. While these tunes are some of my favorites, I do miss the brash naive experimentalism of the earlier Micky Dolenz productions.

Guitarist Louie Shelton gets to show off even more on the tune **"Little Girl"**. This tune fits in well with the previous tune, but is a little more electric in tone. It almost has the jazz-rock feel of some of Davy's productions of this time like "French Song." The lyrics are nothing special, another warning about potential bad girl, but Micky delivers them wonderfully. It's hard to tell how the protagonist's friends really feel about the title character. On one hand the narrator is embarrassed to tell them that he fell for her but then they are trying to him advice on how to win her heart. Once again, Micky cranks up the tempo and then delivers the lyrics with ease despite the speed. The toms in the bridge section are a nice touch and Micky does a wonderful job overdubbing his backing vocals. This is a song that certainly deserves to be rediscovered by Monkees fans.

Appropriately enough, this playlist wraps up with **"Pillow Time"**. The song, which was co-written by Micky's mother Janelle Scott has even more of the adult contemporary jazz feel that Davy was also working in. Maybe the two were co-conspiring to try and make *The Monkees Present* into some sort of adult contemporary album that they didn't quite follow through on.

While the song is clearly aimed at putting little ones to sleep, it also works really well with a more mature and sophisticated audience. Micky even re-recorded this tune in a fairly similar arrangement for his 1991 lullaby album, *Micky Dolenz Puts You To Sleep*. It's a song that is so cute it might've been unbearable had Davy sung it. With Micky's vocal it comes off nicely. It may be a little to finger-snappin' to really help one fall asleep to, but it still a nice, lazy, quiet feel to it. It's also good to hear Micky stretching himself after a couple tracks in a row that were threatening to be a little too similar in style. This would be the last that the Monkees as individuals would be contributing to the Monkees' project, but the Monkees itself still had a little life left to it.

BONES HOWE, LESTER SILL, DENNY RANDELL, JACK NICHOLSON, ETC.

BONES HOWE

1.) Someday Man 2:41
(written by Roger Nichols and Paul Williams)
released as the b-side of the "Listen To The Band" single
November 7th, 1968

2.) A Man Without A Dream 3:00
(written by Gerry Goffin and Carole King)
from *Instant Replay*
November 7th, 1968

UNFINISHED SONGS FROM THESE SESSIONS:
I Go Ape (written by Neil Sedaka and Howard Greenfield)
Wind-Up Man (written by Bill Dorsey)
Naked Persimmon (written by Michael Nesmith)
(I Prithee) Do Not Ask For Love (written by Michael Martin Murphey)
Goldilocks Sometime (written by Bill Dorsey)
String For My Kite (written by Bill Dorsey)
Darwin (written by Bill Dorsey)
California, Here It Comes (written by Buddy DeSylva, Al Jolson, and Joseph Meyer)

Produced by Bones Howe

MUSICIANS:
MIKE DEASY & TOMMY TEDESCO: guitar
JOE OSBORN: bass
HAL BLAINE: drums, percussion
LARRY KNETCHEL & JIMMY ROWLES: piano

CONTE CANDOLI & BUDDY CHILDERS: trumpet
JIM DECKER, VINCE DeROSA, BILL HINSHAW, & DICK PERISSI: french horn
BOB EDMONSON & LEW McCREARY: trombone
DAVY JONES & DON ADDRISI: backing vocals

LESTER SILL
1.) If I Ever Get To Saginaw Again 2:46
(written by Jack Keller and Bob Russell)
first released on *Missing Links Vol. II*
March 9th, 1968

2.) Wasn't Born To Follow
(written by Gerry Goffin and Carole King)
from *Good Times!*
March 9th, 1968

REMAKES RECORDED THESE SESSIONS:
I'll Be Back Up On My Feet (from "Jeff Barry 1" released on *The Birds, The Bees, & The Monkees*)

UNFINISHED SONGS FROM THESE SESSIONS:
The Shadow Of A Man (written by Helen Miller and Howard Greenfield)
All The Grey Haired Men (written by Jack Keller and Bob Russell)

Produced by Lester Sill

MUSICIANS:
DENNIS BUDIMIR, AL CASEY, & MIKE DEASY: guitar
MAX BENNETT: bass
EARL PALMER: drums
MICHAEL MELVOIN: piano, harpsichord, organ
MILT HOLLAND & STAN LEVEY: percussion

DENNY RANDELL
1.) I Didn't Know You Had It In You Sally (You're A Real Ball Of Fire) 2:06
(written by Denny Randell and Sandy Linzer)
first released as a b-side on the *Headquarters/Pisces, Aquarius, Capricorn, & Jones, Ltd.* Two-fer
January 22nd, 1967

UNFINISHED SONGS FROM THESE SESSIONS:
I Wanna Be Your Puppy Dog (written by Denny Randell and Sandy Linzer)
Love Is On The Way (written by Denny Randell and Sandy Linzer)
Sugar Man (written by Denny Randell and Sandy Linzer)

Produced by Denny Randell

MUSICIANS:
RALPH CASALE, AL GORGONI, CHARLIE MACY, & BOB RAND:
  guitar
JOE MACHO: bass
ARTIE BUTLER, BUDDY SALZMAN: drums, percussion
STAN FREE: tack piano, mallets, clavinet
DON BUTTERFIELD: tuba
DOM CORTESE: accordion
JOSEPH GRIMALDI, ARTIE KAPLAN, & SHELDON POWELL: saxophone

JACK NICHOLSON

1.) Ditty Diego – War Chant 1:35
(written by Jack Nicholson)
From the soundtrack to *Head*
July 25th, 1968

MUSICIANS:
MICHEL RUBINI: piano

Produced by Jack Nicholson

One of the last-ditch efforts by the Powers-That-Be to revive the Monkees' flagging popularity was hiring Bones Howe, the man behind Elvis's '68 comeback special, to produce a few tracks. He was also hired to produce the music for the ill-fated and confusing *33 ⅓ Revolutions Per Monkees* special. Somewhere along the line, and for reasons unknown, Bones was kicked off of that project and Michael Nesmith took over. In the confusion, it's not quite sure who did what for that special. It seems likely that most of the arrangements are more Bones than Nez, but it's hard to say for sure. However, severe technical issues requiring the whole special to be shot via remote videotape coupled with the public's disinterest in the Monkees in general and the TV special in particular, prevented any of these songs from really getting finished and therefore I will not be reviewing them here. While there are a few interesting songs as well as some real duds in that project, all we are left with is too muddy or unfinished to properly review.

The two songs produced by Bones Howe that did get finished are of a different ilk altogether. Bones seems to agree with the Powers-That-Be that their best prospect commercially was Davy Jones. These two tracks are certainly in the mold of the "adult contemporary" sound that Davy himself was going for with his productions of the time.

"Someday Man" is a catchy tune that fits in well with Davy's romantic personality. It's hard to say if the lyrics are about relaxing and letting things happen or are an endorsement of being non-committal and lazy. The recording does do a great job of using the drum fill to slam on the brakes and ease into the slower sections of the song fluidly. "Someday Man" is not a terribly great or memorable track, it fits well with both Davy's and the record company's idea of trying to "mature up" the Monkees audience to attract a larger demographic. Or at least keep from losing the fans they once had who were themselves starting to get older.

"A Man Without A Dream" is not nearly as good. It is much more consistently slower, and not half as catchy or memorable. The lyrics are less mature being the typical "I'm a boy so in love" stuff that Davy was often assigned to sing. While it is not as schmaltzy or mawkish as Davy's own productions in the same Vegas/Broadway vein, it is certainly not one of the better Davy-type tracks of the time either.

While Bones Howe only managed to finish two songs for the Monkees, there were a couple other producers who only managed to get a track or two done that deserve inclusion here for completeness as well other perspectives on the Monkees' sound and different paths it could've taken but never did.

Unlike Don Kirshner, Lester Sill did have some musical ability. So when he was hired, he did even try to produce a couple of tracks for the Monkees himself. Despite being the music supervisor, very little of this work was released. The only track that did come out was a remake of Jeff Barry's "I'll Be Back Up On My Feet" that ended up one *The Birds, The Bees, & The Monkees*. Much like the remake of "Valleri" that Boyce & Hart were working on for this same album, this version has a lot more horns but is a lot less effective than the original. While Lester Sill was nominally in charge, the other Monkees were so disinterested in what he had to offer that songs with intriguing titles such as "All The Grey Haired Men" never got vocals.

His clout also was insufficient to get his production of **"If I Ever Get To Saginaw Again"** released during the Monkees' original tenure. The lyrics to this song takes the proud abandonment issues from "What Am I Doin' Hangin' 'Round?" and amps them up by leaving the girl in question with a kid. It is interesting to note that this is about the only time one of these outside producers tapped Mike to sing lead. I guess folks like Jeff Barry or Boyce & Hart just assumed that Mike was busy doing his own thing and didn't want to be bothered with their fluffy pop. Maybe part of Michael's resentment towards the whole Don Kirshner regime stemmed from jealous and not being asked to sing lead. Or maybe he was asked and then rebuffed their offers. I don't know. But it is interesting to think what would've happened had Kirshner encouraged Jeff Barry or Neil Sedaka or whomever to reach out to Nesmith during those early years, assuming he would had been receptive to their advances.

While it's unlikely that Lester Sill had Peter in mind to sing lead on **"Wasn't Born To Follow"** it's probably even less likely he would've had him add banjo to the song. Still when the track was revived in 2016 for the *Good Times!* album, that's exactly what happened. Surprisingly it sounds great. I'm not sure who was originally intended to sing this track, but Peter's older weathered voice is a perfect fit. The banjo melds nicely with the xylophone and acoustic guitar. The lyrics are about as meaningful as Goffin & King's contemporary works such as "As We Go Along" or "Porpoise Song," but are not distracting in their surrealism. This song may have originally been passed over because the Byrds released a version of this on their 1968 album *The Notorious Byrd Brothers*. Still this version is much more gentle and folksy than the Byrds ever would've managed, and would've been a fine addition to their catalog at the time.

Lester Sill did suggest the song "D.W. Washburn" for Micky and helped him produce it. Lester did also get that song released as a single. The single is now considered a notorious flop as it was their first not to go to #1, stalling at #19. While Lester Sill was no Don "Man With The Golden Ears" Kirshner, even he should've known that this song with its anachronistic sound and depressing lyrics about how great it is to be a bum would never been a hit. An interesting album track maybe, but not a good choice for the A-Side of a single. The lack of exposure on the TV show and the deliberately baffling flop of a movie probably were more responsible for the sharp decline in the Monkees' fortunes at this point, but the "D.W. Washburn" single most certainly didn't help.

Another producer that Don Kirshner tried to employ during his was Denny Randell. Denny co-wrote "I'll Be Back Up On My Feet" as well as "The Day We Fall In Love." While Danny recorded a number of tunes for the Monkees in January of 1967; only one of them ever got finished wasn't done until late 1969 when Micky finally added his vocals. This song was the extraordinarily titled **"I Didn't Know You Had It In You Sally (You're A Real Ball Of Fire)"**. Given the song's similarity to "D.W. Washburn", "Shake 'Em Up (And Let 'Em Roll)" and the like; it is not totally surprising that Micky dug out this old track. It fits in very well with those other tunes. However, given the weirdness of this tune and the failure of the "D.W. Washburn" single it's not surprising that more of Denny Randell's productions ever saw the light of day. "I Didn't Know…" barely saw release, only being legally available as the b-side of the vinyl single included on pre-orders Rhino's box-set re-release of *Headquarters/Pisces, Aquarius, Capricorn, & Jones, Ltd.* 2-CD set.

The last song that falls under the scope of this book is **"Ditty Diego - War Chant"**. This is essentially a spoken word piece ala "Zilch," over which some honky-tonk piano has been added. This song was produced by Bob Rafelson and Jack Nicholson (yes, that Jack Nicholson) for the movie *Head*. The version released on the official soundtrack is unnecessarily warped. Luckily, the version that is not sped-up/sped-down is available both in the film and on several different box-sets and reissues. I cannot recommend digging up the unaltered version highly enough. It is a good summary of the Monkees' career, the public's perception of them, and Bob & Bert's feelings about the whole project at this point. More than "The Porpoise Song" this is the real theme song from the movie. "Ditty Diego – War Chant" features lines such as "Hey Hey we are the Monkees / You know we love to please / a manufactured image / with no philosophies". With this mission statement and evenly shared lead vocals amongst the four Monkees, this track would be a great point to end this book. While this may be the end of the songs recorded by the Monkees during their initial 1966-1970 run, there were three reunion albums recorded that I will touch on briefly in the following two chapters.

POOL IT!

1.) Heart and Soul 3:55
(written by Simon Byrne, Andrew Howell)

2.) (I'd Go The) Whole Wide World 2:56
(written by Eric Goulden)

3.) Long Way Home 3:50
(written by Dick Eastman & Bobby Hart)

4.) Secret Heart 3:46
(written by Brian Fairweather & Martin Page)

5.) Gettin' In 3:03
(written by Peter Tork)

6.) (I'll) Love You Forever 3:23
(written by Davy Jones)

7.) Every Step of the Way 3:21
(written by Mark Clarke & Ian Hunter)

8.) Don't Bring Me Down 3:39
(written by Bill Teeley & Glenn Wyka)

9.) Midnight 4:28
(written by David) *(full name unknown)*

10.) She's Movin' In With Rico 3:21
(written by Andrew Howell)

11.) Since You Went Away 2:36
(written by Michael Levine)

12.) Counting on You 3:46
(written by Alan Green)

Produced by Roger Bechirian

MUSICIANS:
MARK CHRISTIAN: guitar
DAVEY FARAGHER & GEORGE HAWKINS: bass
CURLY SMITH: drums
MIKE EGIZI & ANDY CAHAN: keyboards
CRAIG OSTBO & ROGER BECHIRIAN: percussion
MATT HARRIS: background vocals

recorded May-July 1987 approximately

This is an album that sounds exactly like its playlist because no other producers were working under the Monkees' banner at the time. As far as we know, or anyone seems interested, there were no real outtakes from these sessions either. This is Roger Bechirian's vision for the Monkees and it sounds even less tailored to them than the theoretical Andy Kim album that Jeff Barry erased the vocal tracks from and turned into *Changes*. The main problem here is the general lack of interest from the Monkees themselves. It seems as if they were content to churn out any old piece of plastic in order to have something to sell before their unexpected '80s revival cooled. Unfortunately, MTV forsaking the Monkees before the record came out resulted in this album doing fairly poorly on the charts.

Since Michael was not a part of the reunion tour and subsequent album, the only member of the Monkees who seems interested or invested here is Peter Tork, who actually played guitar on his tracks and even wrote one of them. However, he was only allotted a Nesmith-sized two tracks on *Pool It!*. Much like Mike's few songs on their earliest albums, these tracks, "Gettin' In" and "Since You Went Away" plus the live b-side "MGBGT," stand head and shoulders above the rest of the album they were released on.

The rest of the songs on *Pool It!* are forgettable, typical '80s pop that suffer the ignobility of not even being as good as the New Monkees' CD. For those who don't remember the New Monkees they were a TV show/pop band created in the 1980s to try and ride on the coattails of the old Monkees' resurgent popularity. They were really bad and quickly flopped, to become a mere forgotten footnote alá "New Coke".

No matter how crassly constructed by studio musicians some of those early Monkees' albums, it at least always sounded like real people playing real instruments. Here, everything just sound fake. This album does sound very '80s with its big drums and cheezy synths and robotic production. What it doesn't sound like is the Monkees. Although there is one tune co-written by Bobby Hart in there, you'd be hard pressed to recognize which one it is just from listening to. Davy also wrote another song by himself, "(I'll) Love You Forever"; but it is equally indistinguishable

The rest of the tracks don't sound written specifically with the Monkees in mind at all. Rather they are just generic pop-rock tracks that Roger Bechirian was able to buy the rights to that were written for either Bow Wow Wow or Mr. Mister or whomever. None of the songs are really distinguishable or worth mentioning. The worst one here may be the faux-calypso of "She's Moving In The Rico" that is even worse than "Acapulco Sun" from *Changes*; although all the bad numerical puns of "Counting On You" almost make that track worse.

There were a handful of songs produced by Michael Lloyd shortly before *Pool It!* as bonus tracks for Arista's latest compilation album. These songs, including a cover of Paul Revere & The Raiders' "Kicks," seem far more attuned to the 1960s sound of the Monkees than anything on Bechirian's album and shows that it would be possible to make a non-lousy record at this time with this type of sound. *Pool It!* definitely is not it.

JUSTUS

1.) Circle Sky 3:33
(written by Michael Nesmith)

2.) Never Enough 2:58
(written by Micky Dolenz)

3.) Oh, What A Night 3:12
(written by Davy Jones)

4.) You And I 2:57
(written by Micky Dolenz & Davy Jones)

5.) Unlucky Stars 3:11
(written by Micky Dolenz)

6.) Admiral Mike 3:23
(written by Michael Nesmith)

7.) Dyin' Of A Broken Heart 3:09
(written by Micky Dolenz)

8.) Regional Girl 3:16
(written by Micky Dolenz)

9.) Run Away From Life 2:43
(written by Peter Tork)

10.) I Believe You 3:41
(written by Peter Tork)

11.) It's My Life 3:41
(written by Micky Dolenz)

12.) It's Not Too Late 4:03
(written by Davy Jones)

Produced by The Monkees

MUSICIANS:
MICHAEL NESMITH: guitar & vocals
PETER TORK: bass, keyboards & vocals
MICKY DOLENZ: drums & vocals
DAVY JONES: percussion & vocals

recorded 5/10/96 - 8/5/96

There should be no reason why *Justus* is as bad as it is. Not that the album is horrible. On paper this should've been a fantastic record, but the reality as far from that. Unlike *Pool It!*, this album was recorded not to cash-in on public demand, but because all four of the Monkees really wanted to do it. Unlike *Pool It!*, this album has Mike, usually the highest quality contributor, on it. Furthermore, the Monkees themselves wrote and played every note on the album. They are even more in control on this album than they were on *Headquarters* which had Chip Douglas as at least a figurehead of a producer. I was even more excited when I saw that Micky was writing a majority of the tracks on this album. This album should've been great, so what happened?

The Micky who wrote these songs was no longer the daring inventor of such pieces as "Randy Scouse Git" and "Shorty Blackwell" but was rather just trying to write fairly typical straight-forward tunes with lyrics about his second divorce. Micky's songs are almost all unremarkable and boring. There's none of the homespun charm of *Headquarters*. The only goofy behind-the-scenes stuff like "Zilch" or "Band Six" is where Mike yells at Micky that he forgot the crash cymbal at the end of "Oh What A Night."

Many people blamed *Pool It!*'s failure on the lack of Michael Nesmith's involvement. While Mike was back for this album, he only sang one song, an unnecessary remake of "Circle Sky" and only wrote one new tune, the execrable "Admiral Mike." It is great to hear the four guys playing their instruments again. Micky has gotten less wobbly and therefore less entertaining as a drummer. More importantly, these four (or three since Davy's tambourine hardly counts) have not played together in a long time and it shows. While the technology was now available to fix any mistakes and make the whole thing sound really slick and professional you never get the sense of a live band playing together on any of these tracks.

Peter writes a pair of great tunes for this album, although having Davy sing "Run Away From Life" blunted that song's impact as this record could've featured all four Monkees lead vocals equally, but instead comes off as typical Monkees record with just a track apiece for Mike and Peter and the rest sung by Davy or Micky. Peter's cool jazz waltz "I Believe You" is the highlight of the album and features some of the best drumming Micky has ever done.

The lowlight is Michael's typically odd-titled "Admiral Mike." The song is clearly meant as an angry diatribe against the press, but when the best insults you can come up with are "slimy toad" or "stupid twit," the venom comes off as a little sterile. To make matters worse Micky's extremely affected vocal drains away whatever rage there might've been if Mike had sung this himself. Not nearly as egregious, but even more unnecessary is the remake of "Circle Sky" that opens the album. The song has already been done and released before quite well. If you want to hear the four Monkees themselves play it, you can always watch *Head*. The *Justus* version does add another bridge and chorus to the song; which is nice, but redundant. Even worse, Mike re-wrote many of the words, which were already fairly impressionistic and meaningless. These does not quite constitute sacrilege, but it is also adds nothing but confusion. The only good thing about the re-make is Micky's cool harmony part. Still, that doesn't quite justify this recording's existence.

Also, getting my hopes up, just to have them dashed, is the appearance of a song titled "You And I" on this album. Unfortunately this is not a remake of the 1969 *Instant Replay* classic, but rather a remake of the far less impressive song of the same name from the 1976 album *Dolenz, Jones, Boyce, & Hart*. While that album's obscurity does make redoing the song more understandable than "Circle Sky," I was disappointed that this was not the "You And I" I was hoping for.

One good thing about the album is that for the first time, do you get a chance to hear Nesmith as a lead guitarist; and this includes Mike's numerous solo records. While known far more as a songwriter and singer who knows just enough chords on the guitar to strum along to his own songs, Michael actually gets to showcase and flourish as a guitar hero of sorts. He's no Hendrix by any stretch but it is nice to get a chance to hear the guys really rocking out.

Now if only this record had lived up to its potential it would've been a fitting farewell to the group. As it stands now it is merely a footnote even more forgotten than the less pleasant *Pool It!* Truthfully, the TV reunion special from this time period that has never been released in any format is much better than the album it is meant to plug. Unfortunately this is most likely going to be the last ever Monkees album as Davy passed away in 2012. There are always rumors swirling around the remaining three Monkees, who surprisingly did set aside their differences and start touring. While there have been plenty of Monkees albums recorded with only three or fewer Monkees involved, it seems unlikely that we will ever get another record out of them. And so this is how the Monkees, at least as a recording phenomenon, ends.

Or so I thought, when I finished this book back in 2015. But turn the page to see the latest addition to the first revision of this book…

ADAM SCHLESINGER

1.) You Bring The Summer 3:00
(written by Andy Partridge)
first released on *Good Times!*
February & March 2016

2.) She Makes Me Laugh 3:00
(written by Rivers Cuomo)
first released on *Good Times!*
February 2016

3.) Our Own World 2:45
(written by Adam Schlesinger)
first released on *Good Times!*
February 2016

4.) Me & Magdalena 1 [Slow Version] 3:33
(written by Benjamin Gibbard)
first released on *Good Times!*
February & March 2016

5.) Me & Magdalena 2 [Fast Version] 3:49
(written by Benjamin Gibbard)
released as a bonus track on *Good Times!*
February & March 2016

6.) Little Girl 2:42
(written by Peter Tork)
first released on *Good Times!*
February 2016

7.) Birth Of An Accidental Hipster 3:31
(written by Noel Gallagher & Paul Weller)
first released on *Good Times!*
February & March 2016

8.) I Know What I Know 3:30
(written by Michael Nesmith)
first released on *Good Times!*
February 2016

9.) I Was There (And I'm Told I Had A Good Time) 2:15
(written by Micky Dolenz and Adam Schlesinger)
first released on *Good Times!*
February & April 2016

10.) Terrifying 2:56
(written by Zach Rogue)
released as a bonus track on *Good Times!*
February & March 2016

11.) A Better World 2:55*
(written by Nicholas Thorkelson)
released as a bonus track on *Good Times!*
February & April 2016

12.) Love's What I Want 3:40*
(written by Andy Partridge)
released as a bonus track on *Good Times!*
March 2016

REMAKES RECORDED THESE SESSIONS:
Whatever's Right (from "Boyce & Hart 1" released on *Good Times!*)

Produced by Andy Schlesinger
***Produced by Andrew Sandoval**

MUSICIANS:
ADAM SCHLESINGER: guitar, bass, keyboards, piano, drums, percussion
MIKE VIOLA: guitar, bass
BRIAN YOUNG: drums
PETE MIN & JODY PORTER: guitar (on "You Bring The Summer")
MICHAEL NESMITH: guitar (on "You Bring The Summer" and "She Makes Me Laugh")
PETER TORK: organ (on "You Bring The Summer"), banjo (on "She Makes Me Laugh"), keyboards
(on "Our Own World"), acoustic guitar (on "Little Girl")
MICKY DOLENZ: drums (on "I Was There (And I'm Told I Had A Good Time)")
COCO DOLENZ: backing vocals (on "Birth Of An Accidental Hipster" and "A Better World")
JOE BOYLE: lead guitar, bass, backing vocals (on "A Better World")
STURGIS CUNNINGHAM: drums, percussion, backing vocals (on "A Better World")
KATRINA WOLFBERG, CORINNE OLSEN, EMILY ELKINS, & ELIZA JAMES: string quartet
(on "A Better World")
BOBBY HART: organ (on "Love's What I Want")
ERIK PAPAROZZI: bass (on "Love's What I Want")
ANDREW SANDOVAL: guitar (on "Love's What I Want")
PETE THOMAS: drums (on "Love's What I Want")

recorded Feb – Apr 2016

When I finished writing this book back in 2015 I was fairly confident that the book was done. Frankly the possibility of the three Monkees still alive would ever record and release another album seemed extremely far-fetched. But here I am having to write my (first) revision of this book.

Much like the way *Star Wars VII: The Force Awakens* is based as much on the internet's comments on the prequel trilogy as it is on any script by J.J. Abrams, *Good Times!* is definitely recorded and released as fan service. While *Pool It!* And *Justus* have their admirers, both were considered pretty disappointing upon release and have not gotten more beloved as the years have gone by. The main complaint by both critics and fans was that the albums sounded too instantly dated to the time in which they were recorded and didn't feel as timeless as the classic 60s Monkees. The trick was to find someone who could sound retro without making it too pandering.

So the Powers-That-Be hired Adam Schlesinger. Adam's work on the song from the Tom Hanks movie *That Thing You Do* is probably what got him the gig. Adam's work on this album is very similar to his work on that soundtrack. At first it sounds like it should be a pitch perfect imitation of the old 1960s sound, but upon closer listen there is something weird and off there, like looking into the dead eyes of a Stepford wife or something. In fact Adam's production style sounds so much like someone in 1990s trying to sound like the sixties, *Good Times!* unintentionally ends up sounding more of that era than *Justus* which was actually recorded then.

For all of its intentions to sound like "classic" Monkees, *Good Times!* is actually assembled in much the same Frankenstein manner as the latter-day Monkee albums such as *Instant Replay*, *The Monkees Present*, and *Changes*. There's a couple of old songs that were dusted off and finished for inclusion. The title track, "Gotta Give It Time", and "Wasn't Born To Follow" definitely needed vocals added, in addition to Adam Schlesinger's guitar solos. Both the guitar solos are very similar both in tone and in playing, but they both fit in very well with their vintage surroundings. While I may not always agree with Adam Schlesinger's production choices, his guitar on "Good Times" and "Wasn't Born To Follow" is excellent.

Less impressive is the other old recording "re-done" for *Good Times!*, "Love To Love." Initially we were promised a whole new different recording of the song that would just use Davy's old vocal track. What ended up getting released was nearly identical to the original version with some very unimaginative new backing vocals buried somewhere in the mix. I understand that with the goal of fan service Davy had to be represented somewhere, and maybe they aren't any unreleased classic Davy songs that still haven't been released. Still this was disappointing.

Also similar to the post-*Head* albums, *Good Times!* contains a number of old songs re-recorded for inclusion on the album. "Little Girl" and "I

Know What I Know" will be covered later in this chapter, as the original versions of these songs appeared on solo projects by Peter and Mike respectively. It's too bad that Adam Schlesinger felt the need to re-record Boyce & Hart's "Whatever's Right", especially since the originally backing track has not yet been made officially available. Andrew Sandoval's description of it in his book as a folk-rock, Lovin' Spoonful type production replete with autoharp makes the track sound tantalizing. I would rather have heard Micky (or whomever) add vocals to that than the rather by-the-numbers Boyce & Hart styled production. It does a good job of imitating that sound from the first album, but I would prefer to hear Boyce & Hart's original vision for the song.

Many complaints about the previous two reunion albums center around them sounding both too dated and not enough like the Monkees. Adam Schlesinger does a good job of making things sound "sixties," but not nearly as Monkees specific. All of the 12-string electric guitars tend to make his productions sound very indebted to the Byrds. The backwards-recorded guitars show a lot of Beatles influence. Maybe it's because of the word "summer" in the title that makes **"You Bring The Summer"** sound so much like another 1960s band who start with the letter "b," the Beach Boys. The glockenspiel doubling the lead guitar line is an especially Brian Wilson-esque touch. Not that this is necessarily a bad thing.

"You Bring The Summer" is certainly a very upbeat jangly type of song with a production that will bring to mind the golden era of the Monkees. This is a very typical Adam Schlesinger production. The song was written by XTC's Andy Partridge and does fit in with the fun image and romantic lyrical content that the average listener associates with the Monkees. Perfectly fine for what it is; and well-done at that, but doesn't stretch at all or try anything new. The best part of the song by a long shot is the bass vocal "baby" Michael Nesmith sings in the album's tag. It only happens once, but it makes the whole song.

"She Makes Me Laugh" written by Weezer's Rivers Cuomo is very much in the same vein as "You Bring The Summer." The overt Beach Boys feel is gone, and Tork's banjo does help announce this as more of a specifically Monkees tune and less of a generic sixties tune. As with almost everything Rivers has pone since *Pinkerton* there is a palpable sense of disappointment, mostly because it isn't as good as *Pinkerton*. Still like the best Weezer tunes it is instantly catchy and Adam Schlesinger's production fits it very well.

While the first two tracks on this playlist are evocative of the 1960s, **"Our Own World"** brings to mind the 1970s more than any other era. Particularly the sunshine pop you would get from The Partridge Family or The Brady Bunch. This song is very bubblegum, but after two songs that are very light and bouncy, having a track that is even lighter and bouncier is not necessarily a step in the right direction. Luckily the next song on this playlist helps mix things up a bit more.

"Me & Magdalena" is in some ways the opposite of "I Wanna Be Free." Both songs come in a released slow version and a harder-to-find fast version. Unlike "I Wanna Be Free" however, the slow version of "Me & Magdalena" is the preferable one. The harder take of this song is another straight-forward indie-pop version of the Monkees' jangle rock, much like the first two songs. The more acoustic take on this song is stunning and is a great change of pace from the other songs on this playlist. Both versions feature a magnificent Mike and Micky harmony blend throughout the song. The lyrics are evocative without being literally meaningful, making the choice of having Mike sing lead a brilliant idea. The up-tempo version features an instrumental break with no actual solo that changes the tonal center of the song to a different key. It's interesting, but stripped-down version manages to get even more scaled back for a verse that Mike sings by himself which is simply breathtaking. It's no surprise that the slower version of this song is the one that appears on the album proper while the "rock" version is relegated to the bonus tracks.

Despite how infrequent and sporadic Peter's solo career is, he tends to re-record the same few songs over and over, with most tunes appearing on numerous releases in different versions. This is not surprising considering how non-prolific he is as a writer as well as how perfectionist he is as a recording artist. **"Little Girl"** was written back in the 60s by Peter for Davy to sing as a sequel to "I Wanna Be Free." Oddly enough, Tork never attempted it during the Monkees original tenure, but there are bootlegs of him performing the song at CBGBs in the seventies. Peter first recorded the song with his pal James Lee Stanley on the 2001 album, *Once Again*. That arrangement is fairly stripped down and acoustic.

Despite using the same musicians as the rest of the album, Adam Schlesinger's arrangement of this song sounds thin compared to the rest of *Good Times!* The main difference between this version and Peter's is the addition of an electric guitar solo and some drums. The drums are important as this song is primarily in 3/4 time, but slips into 2/4 every now and then for a few bars. In the acoustic version this just sounds like a weird speeding up of the tempo. With the drums added, this time signature change makes more sense. It adds a bit of interest to what is otherwise a fairly slight song. It would've been interesting to hear Davy's vocal take on this, but this is still a nice change of pace for this playlist.

While Adam Schlesinger's productions have mostly been emphasizing the earlier, pre-Chip Douglas era Monkees; but for fans of songs like "Porpoise Song," "Zor & Zam," or "St. Matthew" we have **"Birth Of An Accidental Hipster."** Co-written by The Jam's Paul Weller and Oasis's Noel Gallagher, this sounds like some nineties band's attempt to out-do "I

Am The Walrus." Just think Jellyfish – or even Oasis – and you get the idea. Lots of swirling phase-shifting applied to the vocals. It sounds psychedelic, but are actually anachronistic to the era in question. Mike and Micky split the lead vocals that I couldn't really understand while I was listening to them. Reading the lyrics sheet doesn't really illuminate the meaning behind words much either, so it's not that big of a loss. Just when you think you're lost in a morass of faux-hippy trippiness, up pops the middle eight sounding for all the world like "D.W. Washburn." Better yet, it happens twice, making the section seem less like an interloper and more like an integral part of the song. It makes for a weird, fascinating listen and is one of the most ambitious things Adam Schlesinger attempted.

"I Know What I Know" is a song Michael Nesmith originally recorded for his album, *Around The Sun*. Given Michael's continued interest in the internet and cutting edge technology, he started selling MP3s of the songs for this project as soon as they were done through his videoranch.com website. Given that the last two albums that Michael had recorded, 1994's *The Garden*, and 2006's *Rays* were primarily instrumental, it was exciting to hear Nez writing and recording songs with lyrics and vocals again. (I'm not even going to talk about his supposed album, *The Ocean*, which is really just an audiobook and not a real album.) Sure, two of the six songs, "Helen's Eternal Birthday" and "Smiles Of Autumn," were boring instrumentals of the *Rays* mold. Still the others, "I Know What I Know" as well as "Only Understanding Love," "Life Is Long," and "Love Is The Place" are really interesting and hold a lot of promise. Unfortunately, the last one of these songs appeared in 2012. One would assume that since each of these tracks' titles is prefaced with the name of a month, there were initially six more tracks planned; but as is his wont, Michael's muse has wondered elsewhere and we are just left with this half-finished album.

The sound of *Around The Sun*, much like *Rays*, is very much synthesizer-based. Adam Schlesinger's production of this song is 100% more organic. Mostly just piano and vocal, with an acoustic guitar that comes in after a verse or two and a solo played on the chamberlin, a keyboard instrument similar to the mellotron. While the instrumentation is much improved in Adam Schlesinger's production, the arrangement is a little weak. The piano is just playing chords every quarter note without much variation. I like to think that if Peter Tork had played the piano part instead of Adam, he would've come up with something more evocative and interesting. Still this is a great song with a wonderful Nesmith vocal and some of his most simple direct lyrics ever.

With its audience chatter and orchestral tuning, **"I Was There (And I'm Told I Had A Good Time)"** has frequently been compared to the title tracks of The Beatles' *Sgt. Pepper's Lonely Hearts Club Band*. With its small number of chords and oft-repeated minimal lyrics, the Beatles song this resembles closest is probably "Why Don't We Do It In The Road?", although sonically it's probably closer to Paul McCartney's 1997 solo track "Flaming Pie." This song sounds more made-up than written by Adam Schlesinger and Micky Dolenz. It's nice to hear Micky drumming again. It does feature a sequel to *Justus*'s comment about forgetting the crash at the end as Micky complains that he dropped his stick. This is a fun, simple, straightforward track along the lines of "No Time" or "Goin' Down" and is something of an odd choice to close out the *Good Times!* album.

"Terrifying" is another Adam Schlesinger production in the "You Bring The Summer" / "She Makes Me Laugh" mold. Probably the only reason that those two songs made the cut while this was relegated to bonus track status is because people are far more familiar with XTC's Andy Partridge and Weezer's Rivers Cuomo than they are of this song's author, Rouge Waves' Zach Rogue. "Terrifying" is slightly more acoustic than the other two, which is a nice change of pace; but this still very much in the same vein: jangly, upbeat & catchy. If this song had been added to the official line-up of *Good Times!* it might have overloaded the album completely. Set aside as it is, "Terrifying" becomes a little bit of a hidden treasure.

In reward for being the Monkees archivist/historian/liner note author/tour manager/business manager/etc. Andrew Sandoval was given the chance to produce a couple of bonus tracks for *Good Times!* The first of these is **"A Better World"** sung by Peter and written by his brother Nick. Although *Good Times!* is only the second album to have more than one Peter lead vocal on it, he was complaining that this track was left off the official album. The song features Sturgis Cunningham and Joe Boyle from Tork's side project Shoe Suede Blues and was recorded in Connecticut. The track has a very nice feel to it, but seems more like a Peter Tork solo track than something for the Monkees. Even if Adam Schlesinger had produced it instead of Andrew Sandoval, it still would've been an odd fit for *Good Times!* The lyrics are very sincere and may come off as preachy, except when you really investigate them. Looking closer at the words, it's hard to say what exactly this song is advocating for – or even if the better world it speaks of is something we as people need to strive for or is simply an inevitability. Either way, it's a lovely moody piece with some lovely work from the string quartet on it.

Andrew Sandoval is clearly trying to follow the Adam Schlesinger template with his production of Andy Partridge's **"Love's What I Want"** although this song is not so much the rock of "She Makes Me Laugh" or "You Bring The Summer" so much as it is the pop of "Our Own World." The only thing that saves it from being complete bubblegum is the drumming from Pete Thomas of Elvis Costello & The Attractions. Micky singing a few lines from "Randy Scouse Git" near the end is one of the most blatant example of the pandering that plagued the entire *Good Times!* project, but still it's a lot of fun to hear. This song would've fit into the album much better than "A Better World" would have. Sadly, this is one of the hardest bonus tracks to track down as it was only released on the Japanese version of the CD and as a bonus 45 with the Barnes & Noble version of the vinyl album.

All in all, *Good Times!* is a perfectly acceptable summation of a fifty year recording career. After the last one, I am a little gun-shy about pronouncing this as definitely the last Monkees album ever. But if it turns that this *Good Times!* is their last album, it's not a bad one to go out on. Despite the general lack of Davy Jones, it is a fairly representational example of their work, with all the frustrations and misfires as well as the moments of surprising genius and occasional weirdness that they demonstrated throughout their careers.

APPENDIX

Just for a chance to compare and contrast, here are the Monkees' album as originally released followed by the playlist I put each song under.

THE MONKEES
released October 10th, 1966

SIDE ONE

1. (Theme From) The Monkees	*Boyce & Hart 1*
2. Saturday's Child	*Boyce & Hart 1*
3. I Wanna Be Free	*Boyce & Hart 1*
4. Tomorrow's Gonna Be Another Day	*Boyce & Hart 1*
5. Papa Gene's Blues	*Michael Nesmith 1*
6. Take A Giant Step	*Boyce & Hart 1*

SIDE TWO

1. Last Train To Clarksville	*Boyce & Hart 1*
2. This Just Doesn't Seem To Be My Day	*Boyce & Hart 1*
3. Let's Dance On	*Boyce & Hart 1*
4. I'll Be True To You	*Boyce & Hart 1*
5. Sweet Young Thing	*Michael Nesmith 1*
6. Gonna Buy Me A Dog	*Boyce & Hart 1*

MORE OF THE MONKEES
released January 9th, 1967

SIDE ONE

1. She	*Boyce & Hart 2*
2. When Love Comes Knockin' (At Your Door)	*Sedaka & Bayer*
3. Mary, Mary	*Michael Nesmith 1*
4. Hold On Girl (Help Is On Its Way)	*Jeff Barry 1*
5. Your Auntie Grizelda	*Jeff Barry 1*
6. (I'm Not Your) Steppin' Stone	*Boyce & Hart 1*

SIDE TWO

1. Look Out (Here Comes Tomorrow)	*Jeff Barry 1*
2. The Kind Of Girl I Could Love	*Michael Nesmith 1*
3. The Day We Fall In Love	*Jeff Barry 1*
4. Sometime In The Morning	*Goffin & King*
5. Laugh	*Jeff Barry 1*
6. I'm A Believer	*Jeff Barry 1*

HEADQUARTERS
released May 22nd, 1967

SIDE ONE

1. You Told Me	*Chip Douglas 1*
2. I'll Spend My Life With You	*Boyce & Hart 2*
3. Forget That Girl	*Chip Douglas 1*
4. Band 6	*Chip Douglas 1*
5. You Just May Be The One	*Michael Nesmith 1*
6. Shades Of Gray	*Chip Douglas 1*
7. I Can't Get Her Off Of My Mind	*Boyce & Hart 1*

SIDE TWO

1. For Pete's Sake	*Chip Douglas 1*
2. Mr. Webster	*Boyce & Hart 2*
3. Sunny Girlfriend	*Chip Douglas 1*
4. Zilch	*Chip Douglas 1*
5. No Time	*Chip Douglas 1*
6. Early Morning Blues And Greens	*Chip Douglas 1*
7. Randy Scouse Git	*Chip Douglas 1*

PISCES, AQUARIUS, CAPRICORN, & JONES, LTD.

released November 6th, 1967

SIDE ONE

1. Salesman	*Chip Douglas 2*
2. She Hangs Out	*Jeff Barry 2*
3. The Door Into Summer	*Chip Douglas 2*
4. Love Is Only Sleeping	*Chip Douglas 2*
5. Cuddly Toy	*Chip Douglas 2*
6. Words	*Boyce & Hart 2*

SIDE TWO

1. Hard To Believe	*Chip Douglas 2*
2. What Am I Doing Hangin' ' Round?	*Chip Douglas 2*
3. Peter Percival Patterson's Pet Pig Porky	*Chip Douglas 2*
4. Pleasant Valley Sunday	*Chip Douglas 2*
5. Daily Nightly	*Chip Douglas 2*
6. Don't Call On Me	*Chip Douglas 2*
7. Star Collector	*Chip Douglas 2*

THE BIRDS, THE BEES,
& THE MONKEES

released April 22nd, 1968

SIDE ONE

1. Dream World	*Davy Jones 1*
2. Auntie's Municipal Court	*Michael Nesmith 2*
3. We Were Made For Each Other	*Davy Jones 1*
4. Tapioca Tundra	*Michael Nesmith 2*
5. Daydream Believer	*Chip Douglas 2*
6. Writing Wrongs	*Michael Nesmith 2*

SIDE TWO

1. I'll Be Back Up On My Feet	*Jeff Barry 1*
2. The Poster	*Davy Jones 1*
3. P.O. Box 9847	*Boyce & Hart 3*
4. Magnolia Simms	*Michael Nesmith 2*
5. Valleri	*Boyce & Hart 2*
6. Zor And Zam	*Micky Dolenz*

SOUNDTRACK TO
THE MOVIE *HEAD*
released December 1st, 1968

SIDE ONE

1. ~~Opening Ceremony~~	** soundtrack*
2. Porpoise Song (Theme from *Head*)	*Goffin & King*
3. Ditty Diego – War Chant	*Jack Nicholson*
4. Circle Sky	*Michael Nesmith 2*
5. ~~Supplico~~	** soundtrack*
6. Can You Dig It?	*Peter Tork*
7. ~~Gravy~~	** soundtrack*

SIDE TWO

1. ~~Superstitious~~	** soundtrack*
2. As We Go Along	*Goffin & King*
3. ~~Dandruff?~~	** soundtrack*
4. Daddy's Song	*Michael Nesmith 2*
5. ~~Poll~~	** soundtrack*
6. Long Title: Do I Have To Do This All Over Again?	*Peter Tork*
7. ~~Swami – Plus Strings (Ken Thorn)~~	** soundtrack*

* Note that several tracks on this album are not actual songs by rather montages composed of snippets of dialog in the movie and therefore are not covered in this book.

INSTANT REPLAY

released February 15th, 1969

SIDE ONE

1. Through The Looking Glass	*Boyce & Hart 2*
2. Don't Listen To Linda	*Boyce & Hart 2*
3. I Won't Be The Same Without Her	*Michael Nesmith 1*
4. Just A Game	*Micky Dolenz*
5. Me Without You	*Boyce & Hart 3*
6. Don't Wait For Me	*Michael Nesmith 3*

SIDE TWO

1. You And I	*Davy Jones 2*
2. While I Cry	*Michael Nesmith 2*
3. Tear Drop City	*Boyce & Hart 2*
4. The Girl I Left Behind Me	*Sedaka & Bayer*
5. A Man Without A Dream	*Bones Howe*
6. Shorty Blackwell	*Micky Dolenz*

THE MONKEES PRESENT

released October 1st, 1969

SIDE ONE

1. Little Girl	*Micky Dolenz*
2. Good Clean Fun	*Michael Nesmith 3*
3. If I Knew	*Davy Jones 2*
4. Bye Bye Baby Bye Bye	*Micky Dolenz*
5. Never Tell A Woman Yes	*Michael Nesmith 4*
6. Looking For The Good Times	*Boyce & Hart 2*

SIDE TWO

1. Ladies Aid Society	*Boyce & Hart 2*
2. Listen To The Band	*Michael Nesmith 3*
3. French Song	*Davy Jones 2*
4. Mommy And Daddy	*Micky Dolenz*
5. Oklahoma Backroom Dancer	*Michael Nesmith 4*
6. Pillow Time	*Micky Dolenz*

CHANGES
released June 1970

SIDE ONE

1. Oh My My	*Jeff Barry 3*
2. Ticket On A Ferry Ride	*Jeff Barry 3*
3. You're So Good To Me	*Jeff Barry 3*
4. It's Got To Be Love	*Jeff Barry 3*
5. Acapulco Sun	*Jeff Barry 3*
6. 99 Pounds	*Jeff Barry 1*

SIDE TWO

1. Tell Me Love	*Jeff Barry 3*
2. Do You Feel It Too?	*Jeff Barry 3*
3. I Love You Better	*Jeff Barry 3*
4. All Alone In The Dark	*Jeff Barry 3*
5. Midnight Train	*Micky Dolenz*
6. I Never Thought It Peculiar	*Boyce & Hart 2*

GOOD TIMES!
released May 27th, 2016

SIDE ONE

1. Good Times	*Michael Nesmith 2*
2. You Bring The Summer	*Adam Schlesinger*
3. She Makes Me Laugh	*Adam Schlesinger*
4. Our Own World	*Adam Schlesinger*
5. Gotta Give It Time	*Jeff Barry 2*
6. Me & Magdalena	*Adam Schlesinger*

SIDE TWO

1. Whatever's Right	*Boyce & Hart 1*
2. Love To Love	*Jeff Barry 2*
3. Little Girl	*Adam Schlesinger*
4. Birth Of An Accidental Hipster	*Adam Schlesinger*
5. Wasn't Born To Follow	*Lester Sill*
6. I Know What I Know	*Adam Schlesinger*
7. I Was There (And I'm Told I Had A Good Time)	*Adam Schlesinger*

SONG INDEX

This page left unintentionally blank.